THE
LOGICAL
LAW *of*
ATTRACTION

Helen Racz and
Cindy Childress, Ph. D.

BALBOA.PRESS
A DIVISION OF HAY HOUSE

Balboa Press books may be ordered through booksellers or by contacting:

Balboa Press
A Division of Hay House
1663 Liberty Drive
Bloomington, IN 47403
www.balboapress.com
1 (877) 407-4847

Print information available on the last page.

ISBN: 978-1-9822-4241-1 (sc)
ISBN: 978-1-9822-4243-5 (hc)
ISBN: 978-1-9822-4242-8 (e)

Library of Congress Control Number: 2020902024

Balboa Press rev. date: 02/03/2020

Praise for *The Logical Law of Attraction*:

"This book masterfully serves as a practical guide for understanding and incorporating spiritual principles into our human experience. The most beautiful aspect of this work is its capacity to be applied to so many areas of life. I encourage anyone seeking a functional perspective of the law of attraction to study this text!"

-Courtney Ajiodo, MA, LPC, LCDC

"I used to think the Law of Attraction meant just "feeling" my way into a better life. That didn't get me very far, believe me. As a student of Helen Racz's Logical Law of Attraction courses, I've been delighted to use my mind as a tool to change my experience of myself. I learned to choose who I wanted to be when my aged father-in-law became a housemate and when breast cancer moved into my body. Helen's powerful ideas have helped me suffer less and love more."

-Lois Voth, Mediator

"Are you ready to shift the way you think in order to attract more of what you want and contribute to the highest good of all? In LLOA, highly effective teacher and coach Helen Racz provides valuable information on ways to become aware of vibrational patterns and why the Law of Attraction is logical. Through teachings and life examples, this book brings clarity on how to apply principle-based thinking to keep your vibrations high and consciously create the life you want!"

-Mariela Maya, author of Practical Guide to the Tzolkin, http://mayankin.com

"I know Helen Racz to be a magical being, mentor, spiritual leader and friend. She has an endless capacity to reach/learn/grow/expand and then enthusiastically share and explore even further with those around her....she is a voice of truth, compassion and a most generous soul. As a result of her teachings, I have recognized and transformed many limiting thoughts and behaviors that were running my life on auto-pilot. Her guidance enabled me to reverse course and explore a more fulfilling life with deeper purpose and satisfaction. I am beyond blessed to have enjoyed several years of learning from her live and web-based teachings, as well as one on one coaching. This book will allow those who do not have the opportunity to experience Helen in the flesh, a look into her insights and wisdom which she so freely offers to anyone wanting to take the journey with her. Helen's dedication and teachings ripple out beyond measure and I am thrilled that the time has come for her to share all of this in print...what a gift to the world!"

-Laura Williams

"If you have already developed a strong Spiritual IQ this book is written for you to take all the things you have learned and apply them practically in your life for tangible results. If you have not yet built a strong Spiritual IQ not to worry! This book will help you do that if you read it with an open heart and willing spirit. The Logical Law of Attraction is a process driven formula and that is the only kind that works, for true conscious evolution, outside of a near death experience epiphany. Kudos to Helen Racz and Cindy Childress for a tool that motivates and inspires."

-Peggy Sue Skipper, Author, The Art of Conscious Evolution

"The deep resonance I felt with Helen and Cindy's "LLOA" was the principal of Giving and Receiving. All of my life, both personally and professionally, I have been a "giver". As much as I wanted to surrender to receiving, I continually emptied my emotional bank account by preempting and meeting the needs of others. The principal of Giving and Receiving laid out by Helen and Cindy gave me a clear, concise roadmap of what always sounded so simple yet remained just out of my reach. After absorbing the deep meaning of LLOA I am committed to starting the new decade 2020 by applying the no nonsense principals of balancing my emotional bank account with the same love, compassion and service for myself as I have always given to others. It is truly a WIN-WIN-WIN life affirming endeavor."

-Kay Vogel, CCP, SEP Colorpuncturist and Trauma Specialist

"Finally, a fresh perspective on the often-misunderstood Law of Attraction. A powerful journey guiding readers on a clear, precise, and actionable path into clarity. *The Logical Law of Attraction* is a mix of inspired information and practical everyday applications that will supercharge and shortcut the effort it takes to manifest what you want. Definitely a new must-have classic for anyone studying success and spirituality."

-Doyle Ward, Intuitive Life Coach; www.blissfulquests.com

"Helen's dedication and skill in studying, distilling and synthesizing metaphysical and practical knowledge from a multitude of sources and giving it her own unique viewpoint has culminated in this book. It is the result of years of work and sacrifice. To gift the world with the Logical Law of Attraction – a practical guide to conscious creation on this physical plane – what an achievement! It has been my great privilege and pleasure to call Helen friend, colleague and mentor."

-Alan Anderson, Videographer, Webmaster www.Emissarians.com

"What a wonderful gift to those who have done their work and are now ready to consciously co-create their best life with the Universe. This book is packed with powerful tools to help the reader catapult into the next level. LLOA is a guidebook for the person who has done the inner work to clear blocks and emotional debris and is ready to create the life they desire with clarity and logical steps. The logical part explained in the book is the missing puzzle piece to create masterfully. This book will help the reader make immediate and profound changes in any and all areas of their life. If you're ready to take charge of your life, your energy and your goals this is a must-read."

-Nuris Ocegueda, Business Owner

"Helen Racz and Cindy Childress's book is ingenuously written with all of their readers in mind; it urges us to focus on the end in mind and pre-paving our way to a fulfilled life of our own desires. This book draws on spiritual wisdom from Helen's years of practice and study of law of attraction. Helen moves through these principles with conviction and practical knowledge of spiritual awakening. When you layer in the teachings from the book with real life situations you have had the opportunity to cultivate gratitude, which gives the future self the vision of a divine existence. I am forever grateful and always learning from Helen and her guidance to live a life of love and happiness."

-Paige Manginello

"Helen Racz has taught me how to think through principle-based thinking in the midst of a crisis and I was able to find direction and solution. This book and Helen's teachings have changed my life forever giving me tools to work through every challenging human experience with clarity and self-love. When this life lesson handbook is applied with practice, you will experience the best "you" in every situation....Truly life changing, _a must read!!_ Now you can apply the practical techniques in this book to create balance, harmony and positive change in your body, mind and spirit!!"

-Chere Cormier, SVP Primerica

"Helen is a great teacher, and this book is full of wisdom and knowledge that is earned honestly and rendered vividly through wonderful questions and revealing stories. Helen shares her remarkable practical wisdom, borne of a brilliant interchange of principle-based thinking and the logical law of attraction. She empowers the individual to become an active participant in her or his own life plot. This is the work of great truth and great heart."

-Anastasia Zabelina

"LLOA can benefit everyone and is the missing piece of the puzzle for those who find it challenging to manifest the life they desire. Helen and Cindy have created a magical masterpiece that merges Covey's 7 habits and the law of attraction to logically and consciously create your best life. The dialogue between the two is wonderful and they really break down how to apply the LOA to daily life, from both a personal and professional point of view. This book provides insight into so much, including epigenetics and patterns, and the power of fear, love and clarity. You will come away knowing how you can create huge shifts in your life, and how your thoughts and actions contribute to mass consciousness."

-Kim Shotola, Animal Wellness Instructor/Coach, author of _The Soul Watchers, Animals' Quest to Awaken Humanity_

"Helen is my friend and my teacher. I'm so fortunate to have found her at the start of her EFT journey, and to have followed her as she kept learning and growing in love and wisdom. I've got three journals full of notes from her classes and I'm so pleased to know that it's all in this book now, so that many others can learn how to manifest their best lives!! The book lays out Helen's unique take on the law of attraction – she makes it **logical** - while grounding the reader in the principle-based thinking that I have found so essential to keeping in my own business and helping me gain stamina to choose love over fear more consistently. I especially enjoyed the conversations between Helen and Cindy in the book because it reminds me of my own conversations with Helen. So often she is able to guide me to a more compassionate view of myself and others. Helen is masterful at helping each student clarify their end in mind, and there are sections of the book where she shares formulas that the reader can utilize to gain that same clarity, which is the first step to achieving any desired goal."

-Joanne J. Go, MS Child Development; co-author of *The First Years: A Parent and Caregiver's Guide To Helping Children Learn.*

"Helen Racz is a genuinely gifted teacher who shares loving, transformative energy with everyone in her path. Bringing logic—the often missed or misunderstood element—to the forefront of the law of attraction, Helen explains how to apply principle-based thinking to spiritual and universal laws, thereby enabling readers to use their thoughts, words and actions to become a match for (vibrationally aligned with) what they want to achieve. Helen also doesn't ignore obstacles on the road to success; she instead teaches readers how to have their best personal experiences as they address life's challenges. If you want to attract positive change to your life, *The Logical Law of Attraction* is for you."

-Dulcie Wink, JD, Mediator

Other Books by Helen Racz:

Tell Me Where You're Stuck

Journaling With The Emissarians

CONTENTS

DEDICATION

I dedicate this book to my dear friend and spiritual warrior, Julie Parker.

You came in to do really hard stuff, and you apply all my teachings with self-discipline and tenacity. I thank you for being the catalyst who prompted me to begin coaching and who connected me to Dr. Cindy Childress to get this book written.

Thank you Julie! I admire you, I appreciate you, and I enjoy our friendship more than I can say.

I also dedicate this book to every author who has blessed my journey through guidance, validation and challenge in their generous sharing of knowledge and experience through the written word. This is my heartfelt appreciation, expressed in the action of paying it forward.

ACKNOWLEDGMENTS

Thank you Cindy for shifting from Ghostwriter to co-author to support all readers through your honest sharing!

Thanks to my sons for being part of all the metaphysical learning – I was always in awe of how quickly you adopted the logical parts, when I had to tap so often and work so hard at it! I wanted to give you the self-esteem, consistency, and joy in childhood that I had desired for myself. We did create it all together; healing my childhood pain by the way I parented you!

I also thank my husband for always being my anchor as I explore the metaphysical realm and then ground the teaching in ways that benefit our family and then ripple out. His consistent support of all my passionate endeavors means the world to me.

Dulcie Wink, landlord, friend, student, teacher, editor! I thank you for the second book of edits you've so generously contributed. I delight in all we share as friends and in all our experiences in this evolutionary lifetime!

Alan, you're such a part of the E's blessing us all. Thank you for all the videography, patience, questions and friendship. You I give credit to for the weekly classes beginning; it was your comments after coming to the tapping nights.... We've sure been a catalyst for many new adventures!

I'd like to thank all the weekly students, Thursday Night Tapping participants, workshop and retreat goers, and clients for being a part of the giving and receiving that is my soul calling, there are too many to name and yet I send gratitude to you all.

Those who were a consistent part of my journey and who shared so much of their successes from these teachings, many of whom also helped me on projects in numerous ways, I am listing by name:

Anastasia Zabelina, Anna Nelson, Anne Hanaola, Barbara Chung, Beth Kidd, Brooke Dehais, Chris Bennings, Chris Longoria, Connie Dias, Courtney Ajiodo, Cristine Ostria, Cynthia Gerhardt, Donna Nytes, Gina Long, Ginger Wright, Hope Nordmeyer, Jan McCartney, Jen Donahue, Jenny Sanders, Joanne Go, Julie Parker, Keri Swannie-Talbot, Lara Jayne Perry, Laura Anderson, Laura Williams, Lisa Richey, Lois Voth, Mandy O'Leary, Marci Moss, Maryann Gerity, Nancy Hampton, Nestor Vitta, Nuris Martinez, Paige Clark, Paige Manginello, Pam Gopalani, Paula Lamberth, Rhonda Roark, Sheetal Sheth, Stephanie Nelson, Sue Murchinson, Terie Parkin, and Veronica Bourne.

Fellow teachers and energy workers who specifically support(ed) my health, growth and understanding, many of whom are now my personal friends:

Rosa Glenn Reilly, Melissa Stoilis, Chere Cormier, Kay Vogel, Yamini Bhatt, Mariela Maya, Peggy Sue Skipper, Cherie Ray, Doyle Ward, Dr. Grace Pavlovsky, Brandy Deutsch, Brian Stovall, Dr. Dan Mathews, Susan Coleman, Helaine Clendennen, Kim Shotola, Alana Allingham, Paige Allingham. I've had so much fun and growth with you in my life!

FOREWORD

My 11-year marriage was put to the test over the Christmas holiday. On December 21ˢᵗ, I found out that my husband had to go on a work trip from the 23ʳᵈ through early January, and I was devastated. He was the one who wanted to put up the Christmas tree, after all. Not only that, but he chose to go as the leader of his group, instead of making someone else go, and I felt like he was grandstanding at my expense.

"What about me? What about us?" played on repeat in my mind. And my mind started playing stories of all the other times I'd been let down. I wondered what was wrong with me that I was alone during the holidays. Doesn't that just happen to other people? How do you be alone at that time of year without breaking down? I didn't know if I had the fortitude to do it, yet there I was.

As you might imagine, that didn't raise my vibrations at all. I was sad and angry. We had planned to spend the holiday together at home, since our families are so spread out. I had already visited my sister and Grandmother, so there I was alone for Christmas.

The story I'm telling you would probably end with him coming home and me being cold to him, then he would be snappy with me, we'd fight, and finally we would get over it. But, that's not what happened. Instead, I asked myself what Helen Racz would say to me and what she would do in this position.

That lead me to ask myself, "What do I want in this situation?" Well, I wanted to get through the holiday without getting depressed, and I didn't want my marriage to suffer. At that point, I had the end in mind. I realized that by letting myself stew over the events, I was creating a pattern of stewing that could send me straight into a funk.

So, I chose not to be angry, and I chose not to second-guess his motives. When people asked me what I was doing for the holidays, I stopped complaining and instead said, "I'm going to have a very quiet celebration, how about you?" On Christmas Day, every time any thought or feeling of sadness welled up, I started thinking about what I'm grateful for, and I sent him love energy. I sent him warm, loving text messages, and we talked on the phone. I even made sure the house was just the way he likes it and cleared this one counter that I always seem to clutter, which bugs him.

And when he got home, he was so affectionate toward me! He started doing little romantic gestures like bringing me coffee in bed and overwhelmed me with love. I couldn't believe it. Not only had following Helen's advice kept me from self-destructing, which I expected, but it also improved our relationship. When he left for the trip that he is on now, he woke me to tell me "I love you," three times. We're closer than we have been in years.

Every time I work on a book for a client, they change my life. I am a ghostwriter and have spent years studying being an empath and trying to understand the Law of Attraction and how vibrations affect me every day. Yet, interview after interview, Helen Racz continued to blow my mind. I don't know how to explain what's different in her teaching from what else is out there except to tell you to read this whole book where we laid it out in detail.

There are no unhelpful platitudes, and you won't be stuck thinking, "that sounds great, but I don't think it will work for me." She helps you to laser-focus on why you're not getting what you want and what you can do to change that pattern.

In my case, I didn't change the fact that my husband has to travel for work, or that he was gone. He would have to change jobs, and I can't make him do that. However, I did make changes that strengthened our relationship so we can continue to withstand his work travel and enjoy our lives together. And that makes the work you will do in this book totally worth it.

Cindy Childress, Ph. D.

The Expert's Ghostwriter

Welcome to LLOA

Learning "How" to Think—*Helen*

Early in 2005, while I participated in a guided meditation of going up a mountain and finding a symbol, I got to the top and found an old typewriter. I was confused, because I wasn't interested in writing, although I am a bookaholic, and there are so many teachers who I've learned from through books. My students have been telling me for years that I should write a book so they can refer to it, and when I first considered the task, I knew I didn't yet have enough expertise in what I was learning and teaching. Nor did I have enough interest in writing to pull that off. Fast forward to 2018, and my student, Julie, told me she could put me in touch with a ghostwriter, and suddenly there was a clear path forward to achieve the goal of writing a book.

I want to bless people's lives through books the way other books have blessed mine and pay it forward. Now, after years of teaching and private coaching, I have seen remarkable results with my students and clients and want that to expand out to everyone who would benefit. Most people struggle with the Law of Attraction because all you have to do is be a match for what you want, except no one tells us how to do that logically and consistently. For the past three plus years I've been teaching principle-based thinking from Stephen Covey in conjunction with Vibrational Law and have found that this combination of thought leadership brings people into the best possible experience. After all, we're taught in most of our schooling 'what' to think, so learning 'how' is a new concept!

Consider that the human mind only learns through repetition and by anchoring new information to something it already understands. For instance, think of learning the alphabet—so difficult at first to memorize 26 letters, isn't it? Then it's on to learning the sounds and how to spell words. Then sentence structure, grammar, etc. (Thank you, Cindy, for your expertise in that!) All followed by a long process of repetition. As with language, it's the same with math, where mathematicians start with basics and build on them through repetition until they have the consciousness for higher math. These patterns operate the same way for musicians, writers, artists, businesspeople, and investors—they all use the same formula to create ease and mastery. It's a journey of learning and implementing information consistently.

I realized that the Law of Attraction is logical through channeling. Yes, channeling. Let me back up a little. I became interested in energy healing after a Leisure Learning Unlimited[1] Class (LLU) I took in 2003, followed by a weekend workshop in Access Consciousness.[2] In 2004, I studied with a Tibetan Shaman for a year to learn meditation and hands-on healing work. In 2005, I came across EFT[3] and was hooked. After tapping with Gary Craig's original DVD's, I noticed my eyesight had improved; and I was in my 40's. I was also no longer grinding my teeth in my sleep, and even found I was laughing more. At the time, I owned Fitness Zone, a small women's gym, where I offered classes in EFT to the members.

Members that participated in the EFT classes I offered at the gym showed results so incredible that I started teaching EFT at LLU to reach more people. There were many requests that I offer the

---

[1] Leisure Learning Unlimited (LLU) was an adult education center located in Houston for 37 years.
[2] See Glossary
[3] EFT or Emotional Freedom Techniques (often known as tapping) is a universal healing tool that can provide impressive results for physical, emotional and performance issues. EFT was created by Gary Craig in 1990. See www.emofree.com for more.

"Borrowing Benefits" (which is EFT for groups) more often and for a more affordable price. People contributed to get me started teaching these group tapping classes, and Spectrum Center[4] worked with us to offer weekly tapping to the public for donations only in February of 2009. My agreement was that I would show up as long as the donations covered the room rental. We continued for more than 8 years before the donations no longer covered the expenses, so I stopped in November 2016.

I noticed early in the EFT sharing (with groups and individuals) that I was accessing a lot of information intuitively that I couldn't possibly know. And all the taps were so loving, nonjudgmental, AND informative. Something bigger than me was flowing through me when I tapped with others. I was definitely channeling a smarter, higher consciousness regularly with EFT.

I also began weekly life coaching classes named "Self-Invest" in January of 2010. In classes I often had incredible information come through that I wanted to learn. I literally typed recaps of the classes from audio to anchor in the information for myself and support my students. In 2015, I told my videographer, Alan Anderson, that I wanted to channel without tapping or teaching at the same time. It was SCARY to me at a very visceral level for some reason.

I followed my principle-based thought as a way of living and went all out as a teacher to transform fear into courage, eventually channeling live on Facebook on my weekly EFT Public Nights in 2016. You can find all my live, recorded public channeling sessions on Facebook under Thursday Night Tapping—at least as long as Facebook leaves the videos up. I asked who I was channeling and heard "Emissarians," or the E's, as I affectionately call them. You'll learn more about them in Chapter 1.

---

[4] To find out more about the Spectrum Center, visit www.SpectrumCenter-Houston.com.

Expect to be guided through this book the way the E's speak—through repetition and expansion of main ideas. With each repetition, a new layer of understanding is added so you can connect them all and, if you so choose, integrate them into your life.

What You Can Look Forward To—*Helen*

My students often misunderstand the Law of Attraction because it's easy to think it's only working when you get what you want, and the truth is: it's always working. Although, sometimes you don't get what you wanted. So, what's up with that? In this book, I get to the heart of what's going on when you attract things to your life that you don't want, and help you raise your vibrations to be a match for your best possible version of yourself. We do that by applying principle-based thinking to the Law of Attraction so you will master the *logic* of the Law of Attraction, or LLOA.

Consider that everything humans create on Earth begins with thought. Abraham[5] says to choose the better feeling thought. Thought plus feeling equals belief, and your reality is created through your beliefs. All this sounds familiar, yes? Well, I was led to understand (thank you E's and Stephen Covey) that if I know how to think using Spiritual Laws, I literally align vibrationally to the best outcome by my standards. *Dang, so logical,* so why couldn't I see this long ago? Knowing the rules of thinking means I create the vibration of success when I follow the laws, versus the old repeating patterns of drama and trauma I was raised in and accustomed to. AND, I can teach others to see the logic of LOA when it's blatantly clear that each and every success on Earth by humans includes the same formula and the exact same elements of how to think.

---

[5] Abraham is a group consciousness from the non-physical dimension and has been channeled by Ester Hicks since 1985. See www.Abraham-Hicks.com for more information.

You'll become more consistent with positive results in all the areas of your life when you apply your newfound clarity of LLOA. Once you know how to think and align your bodies[6] with what you desire, you become a better match for your best experience and create new patterns of higher vibrations. Everything you desire that feels good to you is of higher vibrations than you now presently have stamina for. You will identify different vibrational patterns operating in your life that aren't serving your highest purpose and find ways to replace those patterns with new ones that are more aligned to the reality you want to consciously create.

Be prepared for what I call 'grunt work' up front to engage with and be open to new ideas and concepts. The logical aspect helps the mind anchor in the information, and it's a different perspective that I find doesn't conflict with any personal, religious, or spiritual paradigms for my clients. In this book I share all from my love of the spiritual perspective as I believe anyone picking up a book with LOA in the title is on a spiritual journey of evolving into conscious co-creation on purpose with purpose. Welcome, I am so happy you're seeking this information!

If you want more great ideas where these came from, I also wrote a book for those not into the metaphysical perspective in the same year this book was written. It's called *Tell Me Where You're Stuck* and is meant to reach anyone interested in bettering their life experience.

Our Goal for the Book—*Helen*

I teach that when you embark on any new goal, you can apply LLOA to have the best possible experience of yourself in that journey. One of the ways to apply LLOA is to use the four questions for Conscious Creation, which are: what, why, how, and how I'll know

---

[6] Chapter 15 explains the "bodies", which include the physical body, mental body, emotional body, spiritual body, energetic body, and karmic body.

I'm successful, as I discuss in Chapter 11. In keeping with what I tell others to do, I set a goal for this book using the four questions, and I share them now, so you'll know what to expect from your reading experience:

- **What**: To show readers that principle-based thought logically and consistently creates the best possible experience for each individual.
- **Why**: To bless more lives with the formula for more ease and joy in life.
- **How**: Through explanations, repetition, and guidance via examples. Having Cindy create the layout and write the book utilizing my teachings (the ghostwriter part) and also becoming a co-author by sharing her personal experiences in learning and applying the information in her own life.
- **How I'll know I'm successful**: Friends and clients will provide feedback (see endorsements in front pages of book). And our own understanding will deepen.

I found that the best way to achieve these goals for you as a reader is to teach the material in the way that best helps my students. In my experience, most of my students don't get new ideas the first or even the third time they hear new information, especially when there are old ideas and beliefs that need to be cleared to make room for the possibility presented by the new ones. For that reason, there's a lot of repetition in this book, and you will see the above statements repeated several times. Repetition creates awareness, which allows for choice.

Most importantly, examples and principles are brought together. Often the biggest missing piece I see in students' understanding is that it's when you use ALL the principles TOGETHER all the time that life shifts into success by your definition—logically.

How to Succeed—*Helen*

Practice! The more consistently you practice principle-based thinking, the more you create a pattern of higher vibrations that keep growing in power. To practice with this book, continue returning to these ideas as new opportunities and issues pop up in your life. The human mind will only work with what it knows, so as you link the information between what you want and what you've been unconsciously creating instead, you will expand your thoughts to be an energetic match for better outcomes going forward.

It helps to have a consistent protocol. If you have a complex project, like raising well-behaved animals or children, or opening a business, you strategize with your "end in mind," or "big picture issues," gather research and information, and consistently apply principles and actions designed to get you to the results you're seeking. You get help when you need it so you can keep going. You also keep getting more information about how to do it better and better, building on everything you've learned and applied so far.

I have been committed to learning and sharing the fastest and easiest way to success.[7] Principle-based thought, or learning how to think, is the key. The amount of time and energy it will take to change your patterns to create higher personal vibrations in a certain area of your life depends on how misaligned you are now between what you want and what you're attracting. It's important to keep doing the work of LLOA even when you don't see an immediate shift. With practice, you will keep improving your ability to use the formula to consciously create more of what you prefer.

If you're purposeful in learning something new and growing to change a belief system, you can achieve mastery, just like getting a college degree, when you apply that level of discipline. Consequently,

---

[7] Please note that it is never as easy or as fast as we'd like, yet there is a more direct route to our desires becoming real.

for whatever you're aiming for, be purposeful, conscious, organized, and logical instead of being unconscious and hoping it will happen or wondering why it's not working.

Here's a quick run-through of what each chapter covers so you can jump ahead to what you're most interested in right now or see how it all fits together to use the book strategically. Most chapters also end with a Post Note to give you a quick overview of how the chapter's material contributes to using principle-based thinking so you can logically use LOA.

- **Chapter 1: From Tapping to Channeling**. Find out how the E's came into my life and how I made the connection between the Law of Attraction and principle-based thinking.
- **Chapter 2: The Universal Law of Attraction Meets the 7 Habits**. Immerse yourself in the foundational vocabulary and tenets of how the Law of Attraction is logical. This is a MUST READ to understand the book.
- **Chapter 3: Know How to Think with Clarity**. To use the Law of Attraction logically, it's important to practice principle-based thinking in all your bodies, and this can't happen consciously if you don't know how to think strategically. This chapter fills in all the blanks so you can use your mind as a tool.
- **Chapter 4: Clarity Combines the End in Mind and Vibrational Law**. Discover how knowing what you want to experience and how to think about it helps you be a vibrational match for it.
- **Chapter 5: The Practice of Setting a High Vibration**. Take a deep dive into how to use LLOA, especially when you're not having the experience of yourself that you want, so you can realign your vibrations to evolve your current energy to become a match for the next thing you desire.
- **Chapter 6: Work with the Laws of Giving and Receiving**. Sometimes when you're not getting what you want, it's because

you're not giving what someone else is open to receive. Giving can be interpreted more broadly—even giving yourself the best experience of you.

- **Chapter 7: Patterns of Giving and Receiving in Relationships**. Work with emotional bank accounts to balance your give and take and communicate with your loved ones about what you both want to receive. On that note, also notice how the reach of your influence shapes your potential—for better or worse.

- **Chapter 8: The Importance of Being in Your Business**. Ever tried to stop worrying about other people and just focus solely on your own improvement—and found it tough? Here I explore some things that make it difficult and strategies to be successful by only focusing on what's within your control.

- **Chapter 9: Be Your Dominant Energy Intentionally**. You're always vibrating at some frequency, high or low. I show you how to apply awareness to what level you want to set as your dominant energy and the benefits of not going on autopilot, which leads to entraining to the lower frequency of mass consciousness.

- **Chapter 10: How to be Your Dominant Energy Intentionally**. I provide strategies for raising your vibration when you realize your energy is lower than you prefer, as well as suggestions to practice awareness of your dominant resonance. The more you practice managing your dominant resonance, the easier it will become to keep it where you choose.

- **Chapter 11: The Four-Part Formula to Create Consciously**. When you have clarity and consistency in your actions, combined with belief in what you're working toward, you're consciously creating. We create all the time, and it's mostly unconscious. It's time to create your best outcomes for more win-win-wins on purpose.

- **Chapter 12: Clarity and Consistency Create Your Best Outcome**. Find out what's possible when you remove the filter of resistance from your aspirations and get out of "no-energy." In "yes-energy," you can choose preference over judgment, surrender over control, and have a better experience of yourself.

- **Chapter 13: Choose Love Instead of Fear.** Get to know the greatest creative forces on Earth, love and fear. To create higher vibrations, get out of fear mode and choose love by surrendering to a higher power to experience an amazing sense of freedom.
- **Chapter 14: Energetic Legacy.** Ever notice how patterns tend to repeat in your family? That's not in your head. Patterns will repeat through generations until someone shows up in the old energy and chooses something different, consistently, to interrupt the old pattern and evolve it into a new one.
- **Chapter 15: Discover Your 7 Bodies.** Take a cursory look at your 7 Bodies: Mental, Physical, Emotional, Energetic/Auric Field, Spiritual, Karmic and Egoic. Get a better understanding of how they affect each other and operate in your life so you can access them consciously.
- **Chapter 16: Toolbox.** Resources for further reading, education, and tools to help you continue working with LLOA.

In addition to my instructions, in most chapters Cindy shares her experiences as she was exposed to my teachings. Bless her for her openness and facing her learning curve with grace! I also received a great deal of insight as a teacher and student through this process. At the end of each chapter I recap the broader picture of principle-based thought for each topic—using Covey's 'habits' as that already exists and is catchy and easy to Google at any moment! I know that if I have a less than great experience, it's because I dropped a principle, so I run through the list to see which one. This repetitive aspect will help your mind anchor in how it all weaves together. The chapters must deal with one major aspect at a time, yet the true gift, the benefit, is utilizing all of it together consistently.

Planning Your Experience—*Cindy*

It might seem fairly obvious, if you know anything about Stephen Covey, to assume that we would have set a mission statement for the book early on.

Well, we didn't. That's not to say that we didn't have you in mind. I actually start my book projects with a long, detailed look at the ideal reader we're going to address. We talk about what you're going through now and what information you're ready for, and looking for, to solve your problems, as well as where we want you to be by the end of the book. That becomes my compass for deciding what to include and omit.

For most books, that's entirely sufficient, but after we finished the first draft of this book, Helen wasn't satisfied.

"We need a mission statement for this book," she said.

"I thought we had one. We want to teach the reader that the Law of Attraction is logical, so they can understand it and can apply it, right?"

"We want to do more than that!"

"Okay, like…creating a movement?"

"I want to do that, too. For the mission, it should be individual to this book," she said.

I thought through my other clients and what we had wanted their readers to get out of their books that was different from my understanding of the mission with Helen.

"It's usually something concrete," I said. "One client wanted readers to start investing in real estate, another one wanted readers to start a side hustle and make a plan to leave their corporate jobs."

Helen waited for me to continue, but she didn't nod, which made me speak faster.

"I think maybe it's enough to teach your concepts," I continued. "Since readers can take your book and do anything with it, from business to relationships to health—"

"I've got it for you," Helen said. "When you use all the 7 principles together, all the time, your life shifts."

"And I also want you to share your experience learning this information."

You get to experience my conversations with Helen when she gave me insight issues I was facing, as well as how I took the tools in this book and started applying them to my life to make changes where I wasn't satisfied. That's what we want you to do, too. As you read my stories, think about times in your life that match up and consider how you might do something different in the future to have a better experience of yourself.

CHAPTER 1

FROM TAPPING TO CHANNELING

Meeting the E's—Helen

As I mention in the introduction, when I was tapping with individuals or in groups, I knew there was something smarter than me speaking, and I had transcripts made of many of those tapping sessions.[8] When I read the transcripts, I was always surprised and delighted at the information and knowledge coming through. Individuals remarked on how incredible it was that I tuned into their thoughts and history so clearly in our EFT sessions. Some even asked me point blank, "you know you're channeling, right?"

Also, in my weekly Self-Invest classes I would often speak very quickly, and if a student asked me to repeat something I had said, many times I would be unable to do so. Fortunately, I recorded all the sessions and could listen to create the recaps, which I did for many years, educating myself weekly on all the wisdom I was allowing to come through. It felt like I wasn't thinking the thoughts before my mouth was forming the words. I would say something and think, "I want to learn that," or "wow, that's so non-judgmental!" This made me very curious about where those great ideas were coming from, so I asked. They answered, "The Emissarians."

---

[8] You can find the free workbooks with original taps at www.HelenRacz.com and have access to the free audio library containing over 2000 audios of original taps.

At my first big public channeling event that Spectrum Center organized for me in February 2017,[9] a very unexpected thing happened. Different people were seeing different visions around me, so I asked the E's what people were seeing. The E's explained that people were seeing themselves, or more specifically, versions of themselves at other levels of existence. It turns out that I had been and still am channeling higher selves, which call themselves Emissarians. This was so fun to know, as I always had an impression of many different streams of information coming through. I'd imagine that guides were all joining in the groups like a big unseen social hour of spirit guides helping us humans through the tapping.

Another aspect of these live channeling sessions is that almost everyone goes into an altered state. It looks to me like they've all been smoking pot, which I remember seeing as a teen when hanging out with my brothers. It seems to me that when I, or anyone else, channel the very high vibrations that are transformative Divine Love and wisdom, we are affected consciously. I often joke that it's legal, free, and safe. The words that flow through me are those best selves talking to the human versions of themselves with the vibrational language of love and wisdom in our Earth words. Some people on the Thursday nights did attempt to explain it as tapping being a form of hypnosis putting us in that state, which only confirmed for me it was unusual enough to prompt curiosity of an explanation for many. It's profoundly beautiful and humbles me each and every time.

Long before I started channeling, I was obsessed with reading channeled books, like the Seth Material from Jane Roberts, Orin from Sanaya Roman, and Abraham from Esther and Jerry Hicks, even before I truly understood what channeling was. And I was shocked, even a bit offended, because they said we are here to be happy, and I still thought I was here to suffer. Those books got me

---

[9] You can check that channeling session out for yourself, as well as many more at www.Emissarians.com. You can check out Spectrum Center at: https://spectrumcenter-houston.com/

started thinking about Vibrational Law. When I started teaching from a place of vibrational logic, the frustrating limitations and pain from my perception of religion and my family background started to fade away.

If you re-watch *The Secret*[10] after reading this book, you will see that the people shown as examples weren't just doing meditation and gratitude; they were also being active. We don't see the hard work and intelligence that also came into play, yet they certainly do. The comedian changed his career by shifting his energy—and continuing to audition and practice his craft. Logical action on Earth balances with the spiritual world. It's illogical that he would have been wildly successful if he changed his energy and then didn't continue auditioning or practicing and performing. In my opinion, the entire documentary is a lesson about the Spiritual Law: It's not what you do, it's the energy you're in when you do it.

Building on the Law of Attraction—*Helen*

My aha moment with *The Secret* was the scene with the woman paying the bill, and there are energy waves of worry coming off her. I had felt the same with my gym expenses and our family bills, and eventually the gym crashed financially. This happened right after Hurricane Katrina, when three big-name franchise gyms opened within 2 miles and offered more amenities with lower dues. Shortly after, I filed for bankruptcy. It was the most challenging year for me, personally and spiritually. My adrenals were shot, I missed the members and working with others. I cried every day and felt terrible, and yet I knew, at a deep level, this challenge was only happening to bless me and not punish me, if I could just figure out how.

I did countless Radical Forgiveness© worksheets and tapped on myself endlessly to explore fear of success and fear of failure. It was an emotionally brutal time, yet I was too stubborn to give up believing

---

[10] 2007 Documentary by Rhonda Byrne.

that the experience of running my gym had given me more than it cost me, as it had been the most creative period of my life. The grief of all I perceived I had lost ripped open my heart, and in that pain, I transformed many limiting beliefs and healed myself of many repressed and painful emotions. I didn't know at the time that it was my habit of living principle-based thought for years that propelled me to evolve powerfully through that year, though I now see it in hindsight. We locked the doors in February 2007, and by 2008 I was earning my living through EFT—something I could never have imagined possible. These seemingly negative events could have sent me careening to my childhood of erratic punishment, and instead of entertaining those thoughts, I looked for the goodness and saw differently.

Our minds haven't evolved to be in the higher spirituality of creating on purpose through ease and joy in physical, dense form. We have the capacity for that now, in ways we couldn't have before. It is a lot of work and effort to get better at aligning, although it's not personal. It's about vibration and evolution.

It's possible to have a practice of Vibrational Law that's logical, not just woo-woo.

I realized that idea was new. I asked the E's if that idea was from them, and they said it was. The E's are the part of us to remind us that we can come out of suffering. I studied LOA, and yet I couldn't do the vision board or add in the affirmations or change any beliefs until EFT, lots and lots of EFT. It was like I was too full of pain to add in any good thoughts or feelings consistently until tapping made space for change. Others drawn to EFT are also in pain, whether emotional, mental, or physical. The E's seem to have perceived all the suffering in the tapping and wanted to show us how to come out of the suffering, so they led me into understanding the logic behind LOA.

Around this time, a lot of the clients I worked with were looping in the same patterns and just requesting to do a clearing for the same energy over and over. This made no sense, according to how I knew EFT worked. My client, Julie, kept coming back repeatedly with the same problems only with different people. I finally realized there's a two-part process: one, clear the old, and two, put in the new.

During a session with her, for the first time I skipped tapping and went straight into coaching about principle-based thought. On Earth, you cannot just 'clear' anything. You must replace one thing with another, or you'll simply loop back to the old and familiar. Look at everything on Earth; change means things change, not just simply disappear. Energy cannot be destroyed or created; it can only change form. Water will boil with heat, freeze with cold, and thaw again. Energy must be transformed through action and by adding something new to the existing energy. Principle-based thought creates empowerment by transforming victim-based energy patterns into new and more positive energy patterns.

If you've ever read Stephen Covey's *The 7 Habits of Highly Effective People*, you may not have noticed it, although in truth, these 7 habits are also inherent in all teachings from spiritual books. A student requested that I teach them, which I did in a 7-week course, tying the 7 habits to spiritual teachings. Then I started to see that these habits are the life manual that we all wish we'd gotten earlier. After the course ended, the students asked me to teach it again, except go slower, so I offered a 12-month class to blend teachings on the Law of Attraction with the 7 Spiritual Laws that Covey branded as "Habits."[11] No matter how much tapping, energy, and forgiveness

---

[11] It's brilliant how Covey presented the laws in an organized way to fit corporate settings. I will forever be grateful to him.

work you do, you can't lead yourself into the best "experience of you"[12] without changing your actions, which of course begins with how you think. How you think needs to become habit in order to bring about consistency in your transformation.

The E's gave me the perspective that everyone is very accustomed to using the Spiritual Laws in each and every success they create, without consciously knowing it. Learn to see how it's there and already working in many areas of life so you can then use that same thought formula, or rules for thinking, in the areas where you struggle. Logical, right? And so, the Logical Law of Attraction (LLOA) was born.

Using the 7 habits, which I interpret as principles, with Vibrational Law was the key that turned the door to unlock my powerful teaching, and my students' most impressive shifts.

How LLOA Is Different from Other Spiritual Teachings—*Helen*

I was enchanted by ideas about extrasensory perception and was fascinated by *The Sixth Sense* as a teenager, back when it was a tv show. Then, as an adult I got more involved with energy work, which led me to meet lots of psychics and energy workers who weren't happy. I was puzzled. It was like they were both wonderful and not, like they weren't living what I thought they were saying, like my parents being Catholic and not behaving in a loving, Christ-conscious way consistently.

Then, there are many books about choosing love, forgiveness, and gratitude. Except, I wanted them to tell me how to heal and how

---

[12] I use the term "experience of you" to mean your personal experience. This emphasizes that we can learn to make a conscious choice of how we show up for an experience. It's not about pushing away feelings or challenges, but how we greet and allow ourselves to experience them without getting stuck in them.

to have great relationships with my husband, family, students, and community while I was doing that. What was missing from those books were the practical steps that made sense to me so that I could fit in happily and confidently anywhere and everywhere in life while choosing love, forgiveness, and gratitude. As I started to study Vibrational Law and did the logical steps to achieve my positive results, I just wanted more and more so I could create a ripple effect of more good.

Good is only fun if you share it.

I've always wanted to have a positive influence, and Vibrational Law makes that possible. I am a catalyst for positive change only when my students take action. When someone's in session with me and the vibration is high, they're more easily able to align to the best version of themselves, yet that doesn't mean they can maintain the high vibe when they leave. So, they need the logic part of LLOA to lean on, in order to follow through and be consistent when they are in environments that are in mass consciousness or low vibes.

More with Emissarians—*Helen*

Before the E's brought me LLOA, everything I studied wasn't anchored, and I didn't have a link on my end-goal to live the type of happy and joyful life that I wanted more consistently. I would see where I wanted to be, yet the ravine between where I was and where I wanted to be was too wide. It still seems magical, yet it's doable now because when I answer these questions for myself, I find the link that will bridge that divide. Finding that logical link works for my clients and also gives them more confidence to take the leaps of action needed to create the change they want for themselves.

My goal today is to be the energy of total love in human form. Ironically, the more I heal and transform myself, the more I find students who want to make similar shifts for themselves and learn what I now understand. The Emissarians are leading me on a complimentary mission to reach ever-expanding numbers of people to bless and support them in having the best experience of their authentic, unique selves.

I'm increasing my health to channel increasingly higher frequencies and vibrations while living fully in my Physical Body. I don't desire the life of a monk living in a monastery. I want to pay my bills on time, to enjoy life, travel, cook and clean, and to evolve into a higher state of dropping negativity. I want to learn what it means to seek new levels for thriving, without pain being a motivation. I also seek to inspire others who want to do the same and make it faster and easier for them than it has been for me.

To get you started on this journey, the next two chapters help you put Vibrational Law and principle-based thought together with the basics. That's how you can consciously create more good, more consistently.

CHAPTER 2

THE UNIVERSAL LAW OF ATTRACTION MEETS THE 7 HABITS

The Law of Attraction Is Logical, Except for When...—Cindy

"The Law of Attraction is logical," Helen said. "When you follow all of Stephen Covey's 7 habits, which are principles and spiritual laws, you are using the Law of Attraction intentionally to get your best outcome."

My fingers sped through the keys to capture her words, and I nodded—mostly to let her know that I had written what she said. It took several months for me to actually get it.

There's one place in the 2004 foreword to *The 7 Habits* where Covey himself says, "...our problems and pain are universal and increasing, and the solutions to the problems are and always will be based upon universal, timeless, self-evident principles...."

That's where Helen gleaned the understanding that the habits are principles, and from that, she advocates "principle-based thinking" to be the logical alignment to Vibrational Law, which is usually understood as the Law of Attraction.

The first interview we had together included me asking her for definitions of a lot of words and concepts, but because I didn't yet understand the first sentence that begins this chapter, I didn't know how to fit all the pieces of the puzzle together for her.

Some of my mental blocks were because I had some of the ideas about energy turned around, and for others, because I didn't yet know how to apply the 7 habits or principles. I also had some just plain mistaken ideas about why some things I had wanted in the past hadn't gone the way I'd hoped and worked hard to bring about.

In fact, I suspected (wrongly) that Helen was also going to explain to me that I didn't get what I had wanted when I tried to publish my poetry collection and when I tried out for the school play because the universe just wasn't on my side at the time. That I hadn't gotten what I wanted because those things just weren't for me—they were for the kids that did get them. I felt that there were times in my life when I had done all the things a person is supposed to do to achieve what I had failed to achieve. In fact, it didn't make sense, and it wasn't logical to me (yet).

After we wrote most of the rest of the book, Helen and I returned to those definitions and realized they pretty much all just needed to go into another book at another time.

It's fine if right now you read some ideas or information and have difficulty fitting it with what you already know and have experienced. In fact, that's expected at first. Just hang in there, because I know the payoff is going to be incredible.

Write This Down—*Helen*

The biggest takeaway from my book is right here, so grab a pen.

The Law of Attraction is Logical.

That's it, simply put.

I'm going to teach you the formula of conscious creation (which you're already generally using unconsciously) so you can apply principle-based thinking to consistently achieve your best experience of yourself.

If you leave this book able to say that sentence and believe that statement because you know it's true, you got it. Right now, you might be reading that sentence and feel some reservations. What's coming up for you? Are you thinking about incidents in your life where you're not sure how this rule applies? Great! Grab a pen and write those thoughts down. As you read this book, you will likely gain new insights about what might have gone wrong. You can then capture those ideas and use them to help you make different choices and take different action in the future for a better experience of you.

I also suggest that you journal about those times in your life. As you write the things you remember, you might also find doorways that you hadn't seen at the time, when you apply principle-based thinking. The E's taught me that in every instance when I had disappointments and things didn't go my way, I could run through the habits to figure out which of them I wasn't applying and to then apply it to turn things around.

The key to unlocking the benefits of the Law of Attraction is training your mind to run through the 7 principles when you're setting a new goal or when it seems like a plan isn't going how you wanted. Doing so allows you to show up in the best possible way to get your best possible outcome or experience. To learn LLOA, I had to unlearn a lot of limiting beliefs I grew up with. Once I understood how Vibrational Law was logical, I was able to use it and also teach it.

It's important to note that everyone is practicing the Law of Attraction and using some of the 7 principles, although, if they're not aware of it, they might be creating what they don't want, instead of what they do want. For instance, if you want to increase wealth, you might create a lavish vision board, yet not understand finance or only associate with people who have even less wealth than you do. Without that financial knowledge or association with more affluent people, you're not in alignment with increasing your wealth. If you want to create a nonprofit, you might fill out all the 501(c)(3) forms, yet not have any way of attracting volunteers or getting the word out about the great cause you want to support. In that way, you're not taking action in congruence with your goal to raise money for a cause.

If you wonder where the nature of evil fits into all this, you might not like my answer: people who create a lot of evil or pain in the world are also following LLOA, because it can be used strategically to create either high or low vibrations.

Thinking of vibrations, in writing this book, I assume that you've at least read or seen *The Secret* and probably other books about energy and universal laws. Just to make sure we're on the same page, here are some brief definitions of terms I often use and will discuss in more detail later. Check out the Glossary in Appendix C for even more definitions of terms. For now, it's enough for you to know these basics:

- **Vibrational Law**: Everything vibrates, both physical and metaphysical; this includes emotions and ideas, as well as objects, and they all vibrate at different frequencies.
- **Vibration**: Science tells us nothing is solid, there are always atoms moving and there is more space than matter. Everything is energy, seen and unseen, and in its most basic form energy is a vibratory pattern. The nature of the pattern determines the frequency.
- **Frequency**: The rate at which vibration occurs i.e. a "high vibration" vibrates at a high frequency, and a "low vibration" vibrates at a lower frequency. You might think about a radio frequency to envision how vibrational frequencies operate. You can tune your vibration to the abundance station or anger station, and the choice is yours.

- **Resonance**: Two vibrations at the same frequency will "resonate" or harmonize together, and this is how it's said that "like attracts like."
- **Dominant Resonance**: The most consistent pattern of all the frequencies from your past, genetics, outside influence, thought patterns, emotional patterns, environment, and beliefs, either inherited or co-created. Your dominant resonance is your natural unconscious default mode.
- **Entrain**: This is the mechanism by which you either increase (entrain up) or decrease (entrain down) your vibration to be a match with something else.
- **Mass Consciousness**: The big soup of everyone's thoughts and emotions, in which the most dominant ones are those with the strongest patterns.

Throughout the book, when I go into detail about these concepts, I suggest references and share resources that have supported me on my journey, and they're also compiled in Appendix D. If you want to know more about energy and universal laws from a science perspective, research quantum theory and string theory to go deeper into these subjects.

I know from my students that most people haven't read *The 7 Habits of Highly Effective People* cover-to-cover and that even if they have, there are a lot of gaps in their understanding. I get it, because I read this book daily for two years before I could fully utilize it. In case you haven't read Covey's book, or don't remember all the details, I briefly explain each principle here:

- **Be Proactive (habit #1)**: Be the one being reacted to, not the one reacting. Remember that you can be in control of yourself. You can choose your actions over instinctual reactions.
- **End in Mind (habit #2)**: Have a high level of clarity for your target mission, individual goals and your overall life's work.

- **First Thing's First (habit #3)**: Prioritize your activities by what's most important now to move you toward your goal and avoid "time sucks" or drama that's caused by acting in spheres that are not your business.
- **Win-Win-Win (habit #4)**: This is the highest vibrational outcome in which all parties win, which requires a commitment to the idea that there's enough abundance for everyone. Covey teaches win/win in contrast to win/lose. I always add the third win because once all parties involved win, then this is a beneficial vibration to contribute to the evolution of mass consciousness.
- **Seek First to Understand (habit #5)**: Keep an open mind and practice empathy by respecting that other people are coming from a different paradigm.
- **Synergy (habit #6)**: I consider this to be a side-effect or added benefit of applying the principles, especially staying in your business and following the universal laws of giving and receiving. Synergy is an extra benefit created when two or more different people or groups work together.
- **Sharpen the Saw (habit #7)**: Stay in the upward spiral by continuing to improve all areas of your life and avoid complacency or plateaus.

You will hear me refer to all 7 principles throughout the book, and we end each chapter with an example of applying principle-based thinking to each concept. My hope is that as you gain more insight into how the Law of Attraction is logical, you will start desiring to utilize your method of thinking to benefit your experience of you. Practice is essential for mastery, so we will practice together to help you learn the information well enough to apply it in your life.

Principle-based thought creates the highest possible success in any and every situation, meaning as you practice it consistently you become a vibrational match for more success. What people tend to misunderstand or underutilize is that we make the best use of

Vibrational Law to align ourselves with a positive outcome WHEN WE USE ALL 7 PRINCIPLES TOGETHER.

One big struggle I noticed with LLOA students was the misunderstanding of being Proactive. Proactivity is NOT about positive thinking. It's about focusing on the action to create the best experience of you in all circumstances—the challenges of life and also the creativity of reaching for something you don't yet have. Positive thought is often a big part of utilizing LOA for personal benefit, yet some situations are not positive at all. For instance, Cindy shares about being alone on a holiday. Death or loss is painful, and when we are in grief or injury or sickness, positive thought isn't always appropriate. Choosing the thoughts and actions that allow us choice in how we show up in any challenging situation (end in mind) is the ultimate proactive focus.

Throughout this book, you'll hear a lot of phrases repeated; they are things I say most often when I'm teaching or coaching. You'll hear me refer to them in passing because it's impossible to teach one concept without referring to the others since they're all interrelated. I want you to have them in one place, so I listed them here, and they will all be explained fully as you read further:

- Know your four key questions about your goal: What? Why? How? How will you know you're successful?
- Know what is your business.
- Be unattached to the when and how.
- Give what will be received. Receive what is given.
- Energy is transformed when you're in the old energy and show up differently.
- Who do you want to be in the circumstance?
- Consistency equals rate of progress.
- Use your mind as a tool.

Look for places when I use these phrases. Although some of them are similar to popular wisdom, I'm saying something significantly different. As you learn those shifts of thought, think about where in your life you can apply that new perspective. It's inevitable that you'll also remember past experiences and wish you'd been able to apply LLOA then, yet I encourage you to be glad you learned what you learned and then think about how you're going to use that painful experience to bless yourself and others. You can't change the past, yet you can change what it means to you and what you do about it now.

Post Note—*Helen*

The 7 Habits of Highly Effective People is a book written by Stephen Covey, first published in 1989. Each chapter in the book is titled for the habit it discusses in detail. In summary, the seven habits are:

1. Be Proactive
2. Begin with the End in Mind
3. Put First Things First
4. Think Win-Win
5. Seek First to Understand, Then to Be Understood
6. Synergize
7. Sharpen the Saw

Here's a quick breakdown of how these principles work together and with universal laws:

- Without clarity on your **end in mind** you won't know how to be **proactive**, and you can't figure out what **first things are first**. Without clarity on your end in mind, you won't know what will require you to **sharpen your saw**.
- Without **seeking to understand** you can't choose an **end in mind** that naturally creates a **win/win/win**.

- Without learning new information, or **sharpening the saw,** you can't define the **proactive** steps to create something new in an efficient and effective way through **first things first.**
- Without developing skill in giving what will be received and receiving what is given, which takes **seeking to understand** others and **having them understand you,** you can't stay in your business powerfully and be a catalyst for **synergy** with another person. Without a clear **end in mind** and **proactive** action you can't set the stage for **synergy.**

You learn to understand all the principles as individual Spiritual Laws, **yet it's when you live them all together consistently** that you suddenly find yourself supported by the logic of LOA. That means when you feel good, you get more good to feel good about! It's as simple and logical as: like attracts like, so be a vibrational match to success by your standards. You do this by consistently creating success in any and every situation by utilizing spiritual principles.

> "Self-discipline begins with the mastery of your thoughts. If you don't control what you think, you can't control what you do. Simply, self-discipline enables you to think first and act afterward." —*Think and Grow Rich*, Napoleon Hill

CHAPTER 3

KNOW HOW TO THINK WITH CLARITY

Clear as Mud—Cindy

"Without clarity, nothing purposeful happens, and we don't consciously create the things we want," Helen said. I stopped and thought about that idea for a second. It made me think of *Think and Grow Rich* when Napoleon Hill describes people who are narrowly focused on a single goal. But I also wondered what had gone wrong for me at times when I did have clarity, and I still didn't get what I wanted.

As a young writer, I was focused on poetry and wanted to be a famous poet and quoted as frequently as Maya Angelou. I did everything I could think of, like attending poetry events, writing and reading poetry, completing formal studies, joining critique groups, and even leading open mics. Chances are that you've never heard any of my poems. I explained all this to Helen and asked, "What went wrong? I did have clarity. See, it doesn't always work for everyone."

She flashed me her signature Helen grin, and I knew she had something big to say. "We don't tend to notice that clarity is very creative—whether it's negative or positive," she said. I wondered how I might have used clarity to create the opposite of what I wanted, if that was possible. Helen continued, "When you're clear about what you want and clear in how to go about getting it, you will be very successful. This is as true of Gandhi on one end of the spectrum as it is for drug lords at the other end." Ouch! Drug lords are better at conscious creation than I am.

I reflected on how I had been fascinated with failure early on. Sylvia Plath had obsessed over her lack of success, as had many other famous poets from Samuel Coleridge to Edmund Spenser. I had wondered what happened to the people who never made it at all, like all the other Emily Dickinsons whose poems are still locked in an attic or gone forever. And Emily had been too scared to submit her poetry again after a harsh rejection early on. I, too, had quit after I felt like I tried as hard as I could and was suicidally depressed about it. The very thing I had feared the most had arrived at my doorstep.

"I had a Theories and Methods of Persuasion professor who said you can learn more from studying those who lose than those who win," I said. "That it's not what the winner did differently, but what the loser didn't do." That guidance is what had led me to study those who weren't great successes in their lifetimes. "How does that tie in?"

"Most people studying LOA and not getting the results they want probably need to be more centered in clarity and focused on their own business instead of everyone else's," she said. "That is easier said than done, I know."

I wondered if all my concern with others had taken my focus off what I wanted. I didn't want to create an epic failure, but my wonderment with them very well might have. Every time I got a rejection, I languished, panicked, and went into a very bad place. Partly, that was about maturity because I had been so young, yet I also saw now that maybe I had done a lot of good actions, although without the clarity I thought I had.

You Already Have Clarity; Now You Need to Find It—*Helen*

Everything on Earth was and is created the same way, beginning with a thought in someone's mind and then developed through decisions and preferences over time—a thought that was and is developed and grown with more and more clarity. For example, someone had to think of a chair as being something to sit on other than what was available at the time, such as a rock or tree stump. What we conceive of as a chair today, in all its many varieties and purposes, was developed and grown through more and more clarity.

Thus, clarity is essential. Clarity lets you align to the best version of your preferred outcome. Without clarity, you aren't aligning to your preferences. Think of what happens beforehand when a builder is planning the construction of an office building for a client company. The details about the building are prepared ahead of time by an architect—the location of walls, windows, elevators and the location of restrooms. The details may include the design of built-in cabinetry and decorative touches such as marble or wood behind the built-in reception desk. Most key details are set before breaking ground. In contrast, there are people who sometimes start remodeling a home without a plan, and they end up stalling out or creating obstacles that can pile up.

So, for those of us seeking to understand how to be more powerful in our co-creating abilities, the lack of clarity opens you up to many influences that you may not even be aware of. Influences like genetics, mass consciousness, and belief systems can cause your clarity to veer off-course. Thus, clarity is about awakening yourself to being present and to being someone who co-creates purposefully. Clarity also leads to a great deal of self-love because the more you get to know who you are, what you like, what you prefer, the more you develop an intimate relationship with yourself.

And of course, clarity is a skill. It takes practice and energy at first to master it. Most people don't realize this, nor do they realize that cultivating clarity is worth the time it takes to get there. With practice and energy, clarity can become automated. Ideally, you become very skillful in creating your own clarity, so that when you encounter a situation you don't prefer, or a challenge that triggers you emotionally, you can find the best experience of yourself through clarity.

Think of times when it doesn't seem like you're getting what you want as an opportunity to practice clarity. The outcome will depend on what you intend to create. You're already practicing it to a degree in your life, without thinking about it. When you go out to eat, you have clarity that you don't want to cook or do the dishes. If you're driving somewhere, you already know where you're going and why. What most people don't realize is that when you fully align to clarity, you ask yourself what you're doing, why you're doing it, and how you'll define success, so that the universe can over-deliver.

What is it that you want out of the experience? In a restaurant, if you approach the experience of eating out as, *intending to feel relaxed and be waited on*, as well as defining how you will know you've hit that mark, everything turns out even better than you expected. This is even true for projects or things you aren't looking forward to. Because you're purposefully co-creating your experiences with clarity, you lessen the chaos around you, be it challenging personalities or situations. This is because you're not stuck in the flow of mass consciousness or inherited or past patterns. You're channeling through your consciousness with your preferences.

The 4 Questions to Align to Clarity—*Helen*

These four questions are a consolidation of the 7 principles that I give my students as a quick reference guide. It's the fast way once you're practiced in thinking win-win-win and have skill in seeking to understand. These four questions can also prep you to write the ultimate end in mind—a personal mission statement. A mission statement is a formal summary of the aims and values of a company, organization, or individual. Once you run through your thoughts on all these aspects around the area in your life where you're stuck, you'll be in a good frame of mind to continue to write your mission statement for that area.

1. **What?** What is it? What's your goal? What's your end in mind? Use strong verbs to say what you want to do.
2. **Why?** If you don't know your why for yourself and who you're going to help, you tend to lack follow-through. This could be either for a project or an intangible thing. Without why, you tend to drop the ball on presence and slip back into the chaotic thought and habit or the influence of mass consciousness. What values and emotions are behind your why?
3. **How?** What will you do in a situation to achieve the goal? How will you align yourself? What new information will you access and apply? The how can often include tangible and measurable steps of intelligent, strategic and logical action required.
4. **How will I know it was successful?** This is the critical question, the one that will lead you to vibrationally align with the outcome you prefer. This question requires you to identify benchmarks for use in evaluating whether and to what extent you are achieving success.

Use the answers to create your Personal Mission Statement, or a specific mission statement for one of your identities (like boss, employee, parent, spouse, etc.). Here's a format that is short and specific to get you started:

"My mission is to _____, _____, _____

(Use three verbs)

_____.

(your core value or values)

To/for/with _____.

(the group or cause which most moves you)

When I achieve my goal, it will be like _____."

(what will be better?)

Here's an example from myself as a mom, and you'll hear me talk about this throughout the book. Notice that I don't follow the format word-for-word, yet I do include all of those elements.

My mission as a mom is to avoid shaming my children or speaking in anger, invest time in them and listen to them, and be playful and give positive reinforcement. This underscores my core value that we can't get it wrong, although we can always learn to have a better experience. For my sons, I want to raise them to have a healthy self-esteem and be self-motivated in asking for advice. I will continue to gain skills and learn about developmental stages of their ages so that I can guide them appropriately with the least amount of frustration for all of us. I will advise them without personal attachment or judgment, and will be honest and non-controlling so they will feel true unconditional love with respect for personal boundaries—both mine and others'. They will feel confident they can learn anything and be solution oriented, like their father and me. I'll be at peace no matter who my kids are in their life expression.

Your mission statement will probably change over time as your life changes, so this is something to keep revisiting. While I will always be their mother, as my boys become adults and live their own lives, my mission as their mother will shift, especially as grandchildren may enter the picture.

Rolling Up My Sleeves—*Cindy*

I decided to give Helen's exercises a try, which is something I usually do with my clients to make sure the exercise's directions are clear and can guide the reader to the desired result. She then offered to review my work. I was blown away by her generosity to help me and set out to impress her with my clarity.

1. **What is it? What's your goal? What's your end of mind? Use strong verbs to say what you want to do.** *I will be a successful poet with well-known poems and collections people will cherish.*

2. **Why? What values are you going to hold?** *I am going to write the truth, as clearly as possible to reveal new ways of seeing, thinking, and experiencing the world. I will stand up to what I see as evil or bullying and express our common human experiences. The readers will see their experiences in a new way and have fresh language to describe emotions and ideas they have and are unable to express.*

3. **How? What will you do in a situation to achieve the goal? How will you align yourself?** *I will do all the things I did before, except focus on successful poets and feed my attention with winners and successes instead of failure.*

4. **How will I know it was successful?** *I will no longer feel like a failure.*

Here's my stab at the mission statement for me, as a poet:

"My mission is to write, share, and promote poetry that reveals new ways of seeing, thinking, and experiencing the world to enrich the human experience for my readers. When I achieve my goal, my talent will be appreciated by those I am meant to serve."

Then, the hard part. I pressed "send" and emailed it to Helen.

She let me know that my mission statement wasn't quite there. Being appreciated by others isn't my business. The point is that I can use my mission to make sure I'm keeping my aim on target.

"This is high-level stuff," she said. "And, if you want to know how to have an even better experience of yourself in poetry, don't be attached to [other people's] appreciation. Think about having a mission statement that's entirely within your control to bring about and measure by only yourself. Knowing I'm successful as a mother isn't about my kid's self-esteem, although I want that for them. My success is knowing I've been consistent. Think about what that would look like for you."

"Okay, I can't wait to try this."

"Yes, this way you will always know you're successful, even when someone reads your poetry and loves it, and you don't hear about it from them."

"Obviously. That's so logical, LOL." So, don't feel bad if you have to rewrite yours a few times to get it right. I'm a professional writer and had to redo mine.

Here's the final version:

"My mission is to write, share, and promote poetry that reveals new ways of seeing, thinking, and experiencing the world to enrich the human experience for my readers. When I achieve my goal, I will be proud of my body of work."

Post Note—*Helen*

Without clarity, the principles are not fully integrated with the true, uniquely authentic you. In other words, **synergy** is limited in like measure to how much your authenticity is limited. In this limitation the **win/win/win** effect is also limited. We are unique individuals here to bless ourselves, others and the world in our own unique way versus the repetition of what is, and has been, already in existence.

Here are a few quick things about clarity to remember:

- Clarity is necessary to effectively and efficiently understand what you want; your **end in mind**, your goal, your target.
- Your level of Clarity of what is your business will equal your level of success.
- Clarity is the skill to be sure you are in your business and that you can use your mind to strategically understand what would be **first things first.**
- Clarity is respecting what is other people's business, giving what will be received and receiving what is given to create **synergy.**
- Clarity helps you avoid reactive urges and be **responsive or proactive** in a way that aligns you to your desires.
- Clarity is a must to go into bigger perspective and **understand** the situation, circumstance, and/or other people's perspectives, limitations and strengths.
- Clarity is the skill that allows you to keep evolving or **sharpen the saw** in regard to holding principle-based thought and conscious co-creation.

Clarity takes practice to become a dominant resonance. Clearly understanding each individual principle means you can utilize them all together.

CHAPTER 4

CLARITY COMBINES THE END IN MIND AND VIBRATIONAL LAW

Clear as Day—Cindy

After completing the clarity exercise, I felt better about possibly returning to my goals with poetry. In the back of my mind, though, I had a nagging voice telling me that I had tried really hard before and gotten nowhere, and isn't the definition of insanity—doing the same thing over and over and expecting a different result? I asked Helen again about the difference between clarity in action and being crazy.

She reminded me that Thomas Edison tried to create the light bulb 1,000 times before one worked, and he had said, "I didn't fail 1,000 times. The light bulb was an invention with 1,000 steps." I felt like that made sense for a scientist, yet it was different for me.

"Isn't there a time when it's time to stop? Like the universe is trying to tell you to put your energy to use somewhere else, where it will be better spent?" I asked. That was what I had concluded about poetry—I wasn't successful because I wasn't living my life's purpose. I had thought I was living my purpose at the time, though. I have always felt born to write, but I'd decided maybe it wasn't writing poetry, rather something else—even like this book.

"Not quite," she said. "It doesn't work that way. You're trying to control 'how' and 'when.'" Umm, yes, you are darned right I am, I wanted to say, but I didn't because I got her point. I had tried to do what I'd heard makes a good goal, which includes setting a deadline.

My deadline had been that I wanted to have a poetry collection published by the time I was 30, and I had failed.

I failed to win a game that I devised. No one in the world had ever told me that if I didn't have a collection by 30 that it was doubtful I ever would. Or, at least I only got that idea from Sylvia Plath's journals, although I could think of plenty of other writers who never did anything significant until middle age, like Mark Twain, who published *Huckleberry Finn* at age 49. If I wasn't going to be an early bloomer, why should that mean I might not be a late one? She had my attention again.

Clarity in Vibrations Through Consistency and Patterns—*Helen*

Let's discuss how having higher vibrations can help you achieve your mission statement's goals. You want the outcome you prefer and are clear on. You don't control how or when. You do control the desired feeling that you want to accomplish. You can achieve a lower vibe outcome, although if you want to be awake and play a bigger game, you want to be the positive change and not be the reprimand. If you need surgery, do you want the surgeon who's stressed out because of people dying or the one who's able to focus solely on the science, medicine, and skill necessary and believes in their work— even though they can't save everyone? Want to know the difference? The physician who stays cool and focuses on saving the patient in front of them is working from a higher frequency of vibrations.

Again, Vibrational Law doesn't care about positive or negative, good or evil, feeling happy or feeling sad. It simply gives you more of the same energy you exude. So, even if you want something that isn't aligned with your highest self, you can still obtain it, though it's not going to help you up-level or have joy. If you're not sure about the highest outcome you can create, you get mixed results.

How do you know if your goal is aligned with your highest self? By staying in your own business. Do no harm to yourself and others. You'll know when you've aligned to your soul work because your work fulfills you and lights you up, even without 'fame and glory'. Examples: writing poetry for the sheer joy of it, or writing a book for the honor of sharing information, even if you don't know whether it will be a financially profitable venture.

You'll see signs if you're heading away from your highest self. If you're really off track, you won't feel good. If you keep following the wrong direction, you will hit physical exhaustion or sickness, which will make you stop and think. Think about, "What is it I want to be doing and, why do I want that?"

Note: We're not all here to evolve and awaken at the same time. When you start waking up your consciousness and think everyone else needs to wake up too, you're in judgment. The world exists as it is, and when we bring our focus to our business and show up at our best standard, we do the most good.

How Imbuing My Thoughts, Preferences, and Decisions with Clarity Blesses Me—*Helen*

When I wrote my parent mission statement 22 years ago and pondered my end in mind, I wrote that I wanted my kids to have good self-esteem. So, I decided that I would never say "no" to my kids without a reason—using action to support my parenting style and accomplish the why of my mission statement.

Fast forward to today, my now 26-year-old son said to me the other day, "Mom, you know that when you would say to ask Dad, we never lied to you about him saying 'yes.'"

I said, "Well, you probably did sometimes."

"You only said 'no' to keep us safe, so that doesn't count..."

That made me think. He was right. Any time I didn't give him permission to do something, I would explain why. When parents don't do that, and lay down the law, children don't learn how to think, and parents might be letting "Mommy Ego" influence their parenting. When you're more concerned about what others will think, or adhering to social norms and expectations, you can parent based on how you will look to others instead of what's in the best interest of your child. "Mommy Ego" is fear that others will judge you through the actions of your child. It's also fear that you are judging yourself as a parent on how your child is acting. Without that fearful reaction, I was able to proactively set boundaries out of love, and so my noes were received as love. How amazing!

Furthermore, in my parenting journey, whenever I felt my "Mommy Ego" was triggered and I would worry what someone would think of me as a parent instead of what my children needed first, I would ask myself "What's my end in mind? How will I know when I'm successful?" In the end, I am holding myself accountable for how I showed up. These questions made me very clear on how I didn't want to parent, which helped me evolve into the kind of parent I wanted to be. Many books helped me learn the skills to parent in alignment to what I desired to experience.

In your own life and pursuit in clarity, you'll find that the deeper you go into checking your belief systems and the alignment you're creating, the more you're aligning to the things you want in that stream of consciousness. It's like being in a high-speed internet connection instead of dial up, where the connection isn't good because your clarity has static, if you have clarity at all.

When you're in clarity, and take action on that clarity, all the organization and creativity of the universe will over-deliver the Divine Creative Good. It works in reverse too. If you're really clear that you're miserable, sick, and financially stressed, and act like it, you'll get more of that, too.

Getting Clearer on My Clarity—*Cindy*

I realized that in the past, I had tried to create and submit my work to contests and publishers with the anticipation to get what I wanted, but also with fear, dread, doubt, and anxiety. I'm not a mother, so instead of "Mommy Ego," I had plenty of "Writer's Ego." My beliefs had included things like, "no one ever picks me," "I never win anything," "really good writers are only discovered after they die," and all kinds of other ideas that weren't serving me.

Helen also helped me see that I hadn't been putting enough yes-energy[13] into the process. I followed her suggestion to practice gratitude for my ability and the writers I admire, my teachers, my access to information, etc. I also started blessing the judges of contests AND the winners. Another thing she wanted me to do that I balked at.

"When you get a rejection letter, send good thoughts to the contest and the winner," she said. Nope. No way. I cringed. "By feeling badly toward the winner, you're decreasing your vibration to be a winner yourself." That made sense. She also told me to look at those rejections as opportunities to change my energy around them. Each one could be an opportunity to choose something different. If I fully believe I will win sometime, then the fact that I didn't win this time doesn't have to diminish my expectation, and the fact that someone did win should re-affirm the possibility for me.

---

[13] Throughout this book, "yes-energy" refers to the energy of acceptance—what you feel when you say yes to something. "No-energy" refers to the energy of rejection or the feeling of resisting something.

As the poet and insurance salesman, Wallace Stevens, said, "...after the last no, is a yes."

Clarity and Applying the Law of Attraction—*Helen*

Above all else, Vibrational Law does not care about negative or positive, good or bad. It cares only about what your frequency is a good match for. If you're an angry or fearful person, the universe will send you more angry and fearful people. Vibrational Law is happening 24-7, whether you're actively participating or not, whether you're aware or not. Thus, you have to figure out how it works to use it for your own benefit. This is where clarity comes in.

We have vibrational alignments that we're unaware of. This makes me think of a student that recently told me, "I simply want health. And ever since I got insurance, I have had a series of surgeries. I was healthy for 5 years without insurance, and now with insurance, I'm always ill." What a conundrum. We determined that she was running the belief that, "If I pay for it, I'd better use it." Beliefs happen whenever emotion and thought strongly align. Beliefs can be inherited or genetically coded or received from mass consciousness. And consciousness changes through awareness and intention; however, we mostly aren't aware of how those things are operating in our lives.

When you're looking for your beliefs and what consciousness you're in, take a look at what's going on in your life. You might have more clarity through the negative if the thoughts that come to mind are about problems or conflicts. Sometimes you can recreate what you don't like because you're so clearly engaged with the thought of disliking something at that vibrational level. You recreate what you don't want when you're not clear on what you could be creating with your thoughts.

When you're clear on your business, you have clarity on what's yours and worth your time and energy. When you're in business that isn't yours, your clarity, energy, and focus are diluted. When you define your business, it's that which you control. Do I control who is the President? No. My business is being the best version of me, participating in the right to protest and vote, and committing to my best in everything I choose to do.

You're responsible for your experience of you, no matter what the external circumstances. You get to choose how you experience yourself. The more clarity you have about what is your business and how you show up in it, the more good you can imagine. The more skillful you are in clarity, the more the Divine Intelligence can over-deliver to you. This is true for business and money, as well as spirituality. People who are experienced with money are much more successful creating more money than people who happen to win the lottery and don't have experience with managing or investing money. People who know how to think and are skilled in choosing their thoughts are more successful in spiritual expansion and living a great experience than people who don't know how to think.

I don't listen to the news, although I do follow the big elections and seek information to make a good choice. When I vote, it's because I want to honor that women have the right to vote and want to contribute to my community. If I'm at a party and people are intensely engaged in politics, my business and interest isn't to educate or change their mind, or to withdraw and never go out publicly. My business is how I show up, so I don't contribute to the conversation except to be the best listener I can be.

Consider that if you don't like what's going on politically, become masterful to change it and show up powerfully if it's in your business. If running for office or joining a campaign or protest is not your calling, then changing political policies or opinions are not your business. It is your business how you share your opinions and why you're sharing your political opinions, preferably while utilizing the principle of seeking to understand the perspective of those you're sharing with.

When you're crystal clear on what's your business and how you want to show up in the world, your body will be glad that you're giving up resistance that anybody or anything should be different. It hurts to hold on to the idea that something should be different, when it's not in your power to change it; it hurts your biology, mental, and emotional peace. Mass consciousness is the reason that there are so many voices that all want to get on the bandwagon of holding on to what should be different, without the vibrationally aligned action to accomplish it. We haven't yet evolved out of judgment into discernment.

Once you're consistent in not needing validation, approval, consideration, or appreciation from others, you're not a fit for their chaos, so you will fade out of their sphere, or they will entrain up when they work with you. Without that clarity, you do a wishy-washy dance and attract more people with the same wishy-washy vibes. You may get most of it right and feel good sometimes, although you'll keep sliding back into the negative vibes. When you act, think, and feel differently, you transform your energy, and those people who are in chaos won't show up anymore.

I've Seen Clarity at Work—*Helen*

For example, I had a client who was dealing with a narcissist living in her house. When she had put $80K down on the home, he said he wouldn't live with someone without his name being on the mortgage. So, she put his name on the mortgage. When she wanted to end the relationship, he wouldn't leave and threatened to ruin her credit. She wanted to keep her house and have him leave, especially because she had built it to her preference, so that was her clarity.

She came to me for help, wondering how she could get him to leave while keeping her house. I told her she could raise her frequency to become so high that he would leave without destroying her credit or home. I instructed her to practice things I write about in this book: gratitude, forgiveness work, non-judgment, staying in her own business, and overcoming the fears that made her go back and forth. She was consistent in those actions and pulled it off. He finally left on his own. It took a long time, because it was hard work, yet he did leave and left no damage to her credit, her house, or her.

For a year after, whenever she dropped her gratitude practices and got into a funk, he always would text her. It was as if he could feel her signal that she was in lower vibrations. I love this story because it's a clear example of why to choose to stay in higher vibrations. In the next chapter, I will tell you how you can raise your vibrations in the same way.

Post Note—*Helen*

Higher vibrations feel better than lower vibrations. We know that healthy organs have a higher vibration than unhealthy organs. Love has a higher vibration than fear. Consistently reaching for higher vibe thoughts and words leads to higher vibe feelings.

When your end in mind is to have more good in life, in whatever form you're focusing on, then you proactively align vibrationally to the good you already have. Allowing negative circumstances to cause judgment or resistance is being reactive. Choosing gratitude for what is going well beyond the current challenge is how to be **proactive** and supports you vibrationally to align to solutions instead of being a match to victim consciousness. Staying firmly in positive expectations means you are aligned to the **end in mind** you prefer, and can think, speak, and act in vibrational alignment with a good outcome.

Synergy is about staying in your business. How do you want to experience yourself in this hardship? What is it you want to know about you going through this? Synergy is what is created between you and the situation you're in.

The **win/win/win** is that you don't' let reality hijack your chemistry and health through stress. The more you remain **proactive** and in clarity of how you prefer to experience yourself, the more you bless us all with the peace you are creating on Earth.

Seeking to understand allows a different focus and is proactive by having you **sharpen the saw** through learning a bigger picture of current circumstances and how not to take it personally. **Seeking to be understood** from a higher vibration of patience and forgiveness, and not taking things personally, means you **sharpen your saw** in learning what can be received, as well as what communication can be heard and will help.

All of your **ends in mind** would logically be about the best outcome possible for you and others. In reverse, this often stops me from being reactive out loud because I never have an end in mind of making someone wrong—that never gives me good long-term results! I might use tone and firmness to get things moving along, yet I never have an end in mind to be bitter, insulting, or belittling to get something. My end in mind never aligns to acting in lower vibrations!

There's a famous adage: "Pain is inevitable, but suffering is optional." I understand this to mean that when you're skilled in principle-based thinking, you would never pick suffering as an end in mind—you'd shift into solution because you know that suffering vibrationally aligns to more opportunities to suffer.

> "Circumstance does not make the man; it reveals him to himself." —James Allen

CHAPTER 5

THE PRACTICE OF SETTING A HIGH VIBRATION

But, What About When Life Happens?—Cindy

I had already understood how setting a high vibration could work for me when I enter a new situation or set a new goal and set out to achieve it. This made me start thinking about times when things didn't go my way. I didn't agree with Helen that it was all about MY vibrations. What about other people and what they do?

When we lived in Malaysia, for instance, one time our refrigerator broke. I called the 1-800 number and expected help. Because we were renting our apartment, they wouldn't help me and would only speak to the owner whose name was on the warranty. Up to that point, I had not needed to contact the owner. So, I did so. She called Teka, the company, and they had to order the part because it wasn't in stock. I was livid. I felt that if they couldn't fix my fridge in a timely manner, that it should be replaced, or I should be given a temporary one (either from Teka or the landlord) so I could keep our food cool because a functional fridge was promised in the lease agreement.

It took 6 weeks to get the fridge fixed. The first fix caused a different problem, and then they had to replace the motherboard. Finally, when it was fixed, Teka called and told me they had given me a part meant for someone else, and I refused to let them come and change it out, which is how afraid I was they would take the new part and give me back my old broken one. I was so angry that I felt like a wild animal, and it was about the angriest I have ever felt in my 30's.

That was a horrible experience. I definitely hadn't maintained a high vibration even though I started out with one, and I hadn't had terrible experiences with repair people in the past or with the landlord, so I hadn't expected it to be hard to accomplish my goal. I finally did, at least, kind of. And wasn't I right to be so angry not to be able to keep my food cool? Wasn't I?

I told my story to Helen, and she immediately saw where I could've done it differently.

"Do you know what word you used that tells me you went into lower vibrations?" she asked. I shook my head. "Should. When you're in 'shoulds,' you're in judgment."

"But the landlord should provide what's promised, right? Aren't I entitled to be angry when I'm not treated fairly?"

"Well, you can choose to feed the anger and stay in it, or you can choose to get the message of anger and then choose to align to solution and keep a higher vibration instead."

I was intrigued, but not fully convinced. She noted that there are several key factors to setting your high vibration, and I did know what I wanted, which was to have my fridge fixed, so I had started with clarity about what frequency I wanted to set. At the same time, when it didn't happen immediately, I jumped to anger and judgment and victimhood, which are all lower vibrations.

"What I want for you," Helen said, "is to have the best experience of yourself even if what's happening doesn't seem on the surface that it's your best possible outcome." I gave that some thought. In this example, there was nothing actionable I could have done that I hadn't done. I had even considered buying a second fridge, but there was nowhere to put it at that time. In fact, today I keep a second fridge that I never use, just in case.

"That's good, although that's not even what I mean," Helen said. "I'm going to give you some strategies so if you're stuck, you can still keep your vibrations high and bring them right back up if they momentarily slip into downs."

Being in Judgment Vs. Preference—*Helen*

Judgment constricts, limits, and separates you. In contrast, discernment and preference are the energy of live and let live. If you go to the grocery store, take time to evaluate many of the labels and think they are stupid in your opinion, you could be there for hours because you're not using your mind as tool to your advantage. Although, if you find the things you want efficiently and quickly in focus and intention, you have a better experience. Knowing what you prefer, knowing what fits with your morality, desire and code, and staying powerfully in that space is the better way to avoid lower vibrations.

Judgment takes a position of opposition and makes something wrong; it is resistance. We're often stuck in our habitual patterns of what's right and wrong and what to do about it. When you're against something, you're in the wrong energy for a solution. When you have the energy that "I know what's right and wrong and how things should be," that's the same line of thought as a terrorist, yet at a lower intensity. For example, the War Against Drugs is not working, and vibrationally, that's because it's a war, so they're working from a very low vibration that is going to be a match for more low vibrations.

It's tough to stay in higher vibrations when you see things that strongly conflict with your moral and ethical values. There are morality issues, such as child abuse, which is wrong. In such cases, if the disturbing issue is not in your power to change, then invest your time and energy proactively. I'm not suggesting that we turn a blind eye toward what is morally or ethically wrong. We can, instead, contribute to organizations that provide shelter, counseling or services to those who are harmed, as well as counseling and rehabilitation services to those who have committed wrongs. Or, send gratitude prayers to those who provide these types of services. And, if you witness a crime, of course you report it. In other words, instead of focusing your energy on darkness, hatred or what's morally or ethically wrong, show up the best you can in the reality you're in.

I've experienced the challenge of avoiding going into judgment first-hand. On the other side of judgement is the freedom of not thinking everyone should be like you; it's amazing. When I let go of the things I used to think were important to fight against with zero results, I became much happier. Letting go of judgment means not thinking something has to be one way or else it's not working. Embrace the best version of you by your standard.

The key here is to figure out *how* to think, thereby giving yourself the best experience of you. Remember, principle-based thought is the foundation of all success. For instance, if you want a successful business, find out how successful businesspeople do it. Develop your own personal relationships with those people by networking. This is common knowledge of how to do something you don't know how to do, and now you're bringing that common knowledge into a space of personal growth, spirituality, and Vibrational Law.

There was a time when fate and destiny played a bigger role in human lives, and now we're called to co-create boldly, build heaven on Earth, and develop our skill to choose. We have more choice today than generations before. We don't yet even fully know what that means. Previously, you were born into your culture and level of wealth and didn't have much mobility. The skill of choice gives you freedom, which is new in our evolutionary journey. The freer we are, the more we can allow others to have their own experience, which is the opposite of war and prejudice.

Anger and Your Vibrations—*Helen*

Anger is one of the biggest obstacles to understand in raising your vibrational frequency. Anger is always about one or more of three things: unfairness, boundaries not being acknowledged, and trust needing to be restored. Chronic lateness is often the result of repressed anger in your past about things that you didn't see as fair. For instance, if you didn't get to express your anger as a child, it shows up as lateness and even adult depression. I expressed my anger through eczema as an adult, until I healed the trust I lost as a child by building trust in myself. Give your adult self what your child-self wanted to receive: encouragement and validation.

Exercise for Anger

1. Take two minutes every day for a month and use a timer.
2. Set aside the time to do the exercise regularly, not just when you're angry, so you're managing the anger, and it's not running you.
3. Lift a racket, bat or pillow *over your head* to make a big motion.
4. Lift your hands over your head and expand your chest.
5. Then whack your bed or a couch with the racket, bat or pillow.
6. Once your emotional body trusts you to do this regularly, lots will come up and out.
7. Expect some days to be boring and seem pointless; it's not!
8. Expect big emotion to show up, sometimes with big accompanying wailing and sobbing, and adjust to let it flow.

Some days you will feel stupid or silly doing this, and then one day you will be whacking the bed on schedule, and suddenly the energy will surge up so you can safely release those emotional memories. And you will feel freer. If you show up for yourself consistently, you're parenting your Emotional Body, so you have to commit to make the time, even when you don't feel anger, to make sure your emotions aren't running the show.

The point is: Use the physical body to move the energy.

It Started Clicking—*Cindy*

There's no doubt that I had huge judgment issues that were keeping me mad when my fridge was broken. My husband was also traveling for work for much of the time and didn't really care very much that I was so frustrated or try to help me, and that made me even angrier. I was angry that the landlord didn't seem to care that I was without a fridge and maybe that culturally the Malaysians weren't holding themselves to the standard I would expect in America, because if my fridge had gone out in Bayou Shadows, the apartment complex I used to live in, it would have been fixed or replaced within a day or two tops.

Maybe some of my anger was not just judging the landlord and Teka, but also pent-up frustration about my circumstances. I was also fighting an eating disorder, and the disruption to my food norms was very upsetting and hard to deal with. I felt powerless, it definitely would have helped to do Helen's anger exercise and let that steam out instead of feeding the residual anger. Then, my mind turned to other times that I could have chosen to feel differently when something wasn't going the way I wanted. That brought me to think of when I had back surgery on a severely herniated L-5.

"Okay, so I can see how judgment and anger have worked in my life. Is the deal that the only time we should feel bad is when something really hurts, like when I had back spasms?"

"Let's talk about that. Why do you think you should feel bad?"

"I mean, when my back went out and I was laying on the floor, I was in so much pain I couldn't even scoot myself across the floor, I didn't choose that. The pain simply happened."

"I see. I'm going to challenge you. Consider, that maybe you could choose to stay in a high vibrational frequency even if physical pain is present."

I was intrigued and got my pen ready to take notes on what she said next.

Pain and High Vibrations—*Helen*

Another time when it's tough to maintain high vibrations is when your body is giving you pain signals. When you're in pain, it's even more important to cultivate and maintain high vibrations to make your body an atmosphere for healing. That's about using the pain to be motivated to learn more and then committing to consistent action to bring about relief. It's so easy to start feeding negative thoughts of how bad the pain is, and then you might start thinking of other times you were in pain and get worried or depressed about what poor health you are experiencing. That will create more of the same.

The next time you're in pain, view it as an opportunity to practice gratitude for all good health. Doing so will be counter-intuitive at first, and by showing up in the feeling of pain and transforming victim consciousness with vibrations of wellness, you will eventually no longer be a match for that pain. As mentioned previously, if the pain has been chronic or is inherited, you will have to do more work to change that pattern than if it is a sudden, acute issue you're dealing with for the first time; in both cases, you can change the energy of your circumstances instead of being controlled by them.

I have a student who had a very badly sprained ankle, and to speed her healing, she redefined her pain by saying to her ankle, "I feel you healing." That perspective was transformative and helped her move through that experience faster and with gratitude.

Set A High-Vibe Outcome—*Helen*

Be in the consciousness of what feels better and better. Even "less bad" feels better than bad, so what's the ripple effect of a "less bad" outcome? Is it going to give you the end-result that you want? Prioritize setting a high-vibe outcome. Someone can talk all day long about how they want to write their mission statement and gain clarity, and until they prioritize it, they won't do it. If you change that statement "I really want to but I'm too busy, I don't have enough time" to "of course I have plenty of time to write my mission statement," your chosen thought will eventually reorganize your mind and actions.

The universe has a way of showing you when you're ready to evolve or expand in your capacity for good. You might feel bad about something that happened or be injured or ill. These are all invitations to choose a different thought and action, to have a different experience. Another sign that you're leveling up is when you might encounter all types of new opportunities at the same time. When you are at a really high vibrational frequency, you can choose your opportunities and lessons to level up and expand in your capacity for good. A thriving consciousness is one you choose on purpose because it feels good to choose.

Choosing "love" over "fear" is the bottom line of raising your vibrations, and we'll talk about this in more detail later in the book. Right now, I want you to think about this concept: How do you want to experience you? Your experience of yourself can be full of love, wealth, and health; or rejection, poverty, and illness—or anything between these extremes. You have to keep using your mind as a tool to be a match for the experience of yourself that you want. Everything is about consciousness, and every form of consciousness wants to be the best form of itself. We can get bogged down in old emotions and patterns that don't serve us. If we're not constantly learning, we don't keep up-leveling.

Higher vibrations feel better, while lower vibrations feel worse. If you're triggered to a lower frequency, you can choose the perspective that will determine how you feel. You can also ask what you're doing to contribute to the frequency. Are you feeding the low vibration or the possibility of a higher frequency? What creative action can you take to reset your dominant energy and rise above the undue influence? If you respond with kindness when someone else is cruel, or forgive, you will end up in a higher vibration of forgiveness instead of a victim-vibration.

In a challenging situation where you struggle to avoid low vibes, continue to choose to reflect and cultivate self-awareness. What is it that really bothers you in a situation? Why? Consider the clarity and vibrational resonance of someone running a marathon with a prosthetic limb who refuses to let the loss of that limb prevent him from having the experience of running. If he's stuck in what others will think or how hard it is for him to run, then he won't run or won't be able to finish.

With logic, the mind can link this information to other things. The current calling on Earth is for us to evolve into better choices. It's never what we do; it's the energy in which we do it. We filter everything through our own energy. People respond to energy, whether consciously or unconsciously.

Your mind will not let in what you're not a match for in consciousness, which is another function of clarity. If you think recovery has to be hard, you won't perceive benefits you don't suffer for. Think about that for a second. Sometimes, it's not that you don't have what you want. Instead, it's that you aren't seeing it clearly to realize you have it, like the classic movie, *It's a Wonderful Life*. When George wants to kill himself, he thinks he doesn't have what he wants and that he failed at what he set out to do. Then Clarence, the angel, shows him that he does in fact have everything he wanted. When the movie ends, George's life doesn't change—his perspective about it does.

Align your consciousness so the Divine will give you what you want, or even better than what you could think of. It's not that things are withheld from us. It's simply that our consciousness might not be aligned to accept it. If you get a job with vacation, travel, and great pay, and you're not used to receiving well, you might blow the good thing that came into your life.

If you're coming in late, playing on the internet at work, and blaming your employer when your performance is found to be lacking, you're not a match for a perfect job. If you are showing up at work and doing the job you have to the best of your ability, you are a match for a better job that aligns you to what you want.

On Earth, you can never be in a vacuum with your vibrations. You have to be evolving to transform energy you don't want more of into energy you do want more of. You can use the mind as a tool to say, "I'm going to give up this to get that." For weight loss, "I'm going to give up some foods and add other foods in." For writing my book, "I'm going to transform money, energy, and fear; and I get to choose courage, education, and faith." What's the exchange? If I want happiness, then I need to quit being mesmerized with sadness. Do your job of clarity in your intentions so that it's easier to relax and let go after you've looked at it from every direction; give it up to get something bigger than you.

Post Note—*Helen*

When giving, or helping another, a healthy **end in mind** is that we want to feel good in the giving and have the receiver feel good, too.

Being **proactive** to understand what is desired by another, which would be putting **first things first**, means you can create a **win/win/win**. You feel good, they feel good and it definitely ripples out!

Without **seeking to understand** what can be received or the timing of it, we leave out the chance to **sharpen the saw** with a higher level of clarity of our **end in mind**. Watch any movie, and notice how often so much communication drama and trauma could be avoided if strategic timing were used, which includes strong skill in being in your own business, which is a must for creating **synergy**. How you give—as in what, when and where—is your business.

CHAPTER 6

WORK WITH THE LAWS OF GIVING AND RECEIVING

Finally, Something I Understand!—Cindy

When we got to the Laws of Giving and Receiving and Helen started laying out the ideas, I was glad that, for the first time, what I thought I knew was pretty much the case. I understood these laws because her client, Julie, had already helped me with a situation in which I hadn't been following these rules, and her help saved a friendship for me. I told Helen what had happened.

The friend was an immigrant to the U.S. and had a temporary visa, but she wanted to stay here. One way to do that would be to get a job and have the employer get her a green card, so she was job searching. She has an advanced degree and ambitious professional goals, so all her friends in the U.S. tried to help her, including me. At first, I only gave her job search support, but as the months stretched on, I started trying to find her jobs myself and would give her every lead that I found for which she might be qualified. I had another friend who agreed to hire her, and she turned the job down. I was stunned and hurt that she refused my help, and it was starting to affect our friendship.

Julie is a face reader and told me that based on my friend's face, she wants to do things for herself, and my help won't be well-received, so if I want to continue the friendship, what my friend would like from others is to feel supported and heard.

"That's exactly right," Helen said. "Julie knew from your friend's face what you could give your friend that she would receive well. It's awesome to have a face reader in your network, and even if you don't, by seeing that your friend didn't want your help, you could have learned from that what she would and wouldn't accept and have adapted accordingly."

I considered that I'd been hurt and upset by what I perceived as my friend's stubbornness and ingratitude until Julie explained my friend's personality to me. "Is there a way then to avoid getting hurt when you give someone something in a way that doesn't work for them?"

"Is there ever!"

Helen explained that when you give something and don't get the grateful reaction you hoped for, or no matter how much you give, they only take and never seem to improve their circumstances, these scenarios are avoidable.

"Aside from reading her face," I said, "how could I avoid giving help that isn't wanted?"

"Things like what happened with your friend and her job search happen because, on an energetic level, the giver and receiver don't share a vibrational frequency and clarity about the end result."

"Okay, like I had found my friend 'a job,' but it didn't match to her end result."

"Yes. If the receiver isn't a match for your gift, it's not going to go the way you intend. And in the reverse, if you're not already at a vibrational frequency so you can be given what you desire, then that's not going to happen, or if you do get it, you won't keep it."

I nodded. I had never thought of being an energetic match for things, but the idea made sense.

"On the other hand, when you work with the Laws of Giving and Receiving, you can get what you want and give it to others as well."

Before You Give, Ask What to Give—*Helen*

To work with the laws of giving and receiving, ask what to give before you give, so that you only give what will be received. This relates to the overall principle of staying in your own business in all interactions. You might be so consumed by your drive to help that you don't listen to the person you're trying to help. Honestly, I've struggled with this some. People like me, who can be a little overenthusiastic, can try to give you information that isn't wanted. I want to coach you, yet you don't want coaching. I want to share healing information with you, and you don't want it.

That's why I have a rule: I don't offer advice to those around me unless they ask me for my help and expertise. With my husband or my kids, colleagues or friends, I pay attention to the context. If you're in my class or a private session, you've already said that you want my help simply by presenting yourself in that situation. On the other hand, if we're at lunch, and you're whining and complaining, I will carefully ask this question: "Hang on a second, are you asking for my advice, my opinion, or are you venting?"

Two things happen when I do this: 1) the person has to stop and think about their intention in sharing whatever they're sharing; and 2) they tell me what they want and energetically align to be in receiving mode. And I will deliver! My kids might want me to coach them or they'll want me to simply be a mom. Or they'll say, no, don't say anything, listen. I only give what will be received, and I know what will be received because they told me. A total win-win-win.

I prefer not to blatantly tell a person what to do, and instead I help them figure it out for themselves. Nobody needs to be me except me, so I try not to advise people according to what I would personally do or want. Still, I will tell them to hit the target they have for themselves. This sounds logical, and it is, although it's not easy, especially when you try to apply it in an area that doesn't feel good. The trick is to unlearn the old pattern of searching for the established answer.

Your capacity to receive, good or bad, is always based on your filters and your perceptions, which are your belief systems. In that way, your perception of reality dictates what you can receive. On a spiritual journey, if you're coming out of fear and choosing love, it will always connect you. Love connects; fear separates.

For example, I believe that my husband and I can be different individuals while creating a great life system as partners that speaks to my belief system of synergy, and I open to give and receive it with him. This unites us. On the other hand, if I have a different belief and think everyone has to think like me or they can't be in relationships with me, that's conditional love. It's based on fear. It separates us and prevents me from receiving love from anyone who isn't like me.

Conditional love stems from a fear-based belief system we learn as children when the love we receive is conditional. As a child, you are very aware that you are dependent on your parents for everything. They feed you, clothe you, shelter you, and drive you everywhere. You can't leave them because you need them for survival. So, when you misinterpret their actions and take them personally, or you compromise your truth, because if you don't, you're going to pay a painful price, then you learn that love is very conditional. Or even learn that love means fighting, or anger, because those were your first experiences of it. So, whatever beliefs and filters you have running from a child's perception of life experiences, you will project them on to sports teams, politics, and even marriage. As within, so without.

Patterns, like familial struggles, repeat if they're not interrupted, transformed, and evolved. Being fear-based, conditional love is a lower vibration frequency than unconditional love, and to be a match to give and receive unconditional love, you need to evolve your energy.

Feed Your Mind to Receive Your Best Possible Outcomes—*Helen*

To get something that you don't already have, you have to change your mind and your energy to become a match to receive it. The first step is to gather information because the human mind can't give you something new without new information. In order to make progress, you have to feed your mind. When you want to be happy or have a great relationship, you have to gather information, so you don't repeat the mistakes of the past.

Positive change, or solution perspective, is not found when resonating in the pain of the problem or challenge. Empowerment doesn't happen from a victim consciousness. If you are consistently feeling like you're not receiving what you want, or are repeating patterns that don't feel good, and find you are just giving and giving, you probably need to gather new information for your progress. This doesn't mean you're stupid or slow; you're missing a piece of information, which most likely is: what is the other party willing to receive or give? Many people trying to use LOA are missing crucial bits of information, especially when it comes to communication, emotional intelligence, and money, so they're not applying it logically. Look for good books, courses, and mentors to fill in in your gaps.

You can also find someone who's already living the way you want and ask them how they are successful, which is what Covey did. Find someone who is facing or has faced the same obstacle that you are, and who got through it well. If you're a parent dealing with an adult child who's living at home and you feel like you're giving too much, ask a friend in the same situation who's handling it in a balanced way.

If you feel like you're being taken advantage of at work and doing everyone's grunt work with no recognition, look for someone else in the office who is doing good work and being recognized.

Ask yourself some introspective questions such as:

- Who's done the journey that you want to take?
- Who has evidence of the results you want?

There are also certain resources you should not consult. If someone is not emulating the kind of life you seek, politely decline to use their advice. For example, don't take relationship advice from someone unhappy in their relationships, and don't take money advice from someone who doesn't have their finances in order.

While seeking information is a very helpful process, it's far too easy to tell yourself that you're working towards your goal when you're actually not. You can avoid stalling out in seeking information by using the mind as a tool, so you're not paralyzed by research. You don't want to be a workshop-junkie or a reader who hasn't incorporated the knowledge. Too often, people are aware they're in codependent or otherwise inequitable or unhealthy relationships, and they binge on analysis without actually doing anything. Study the information and make it your own, in your own words and actions, to integrate it.

Once you receive new information, you can transform it into knowledge by both applying it in a measurable and tangible way. Practicing that application repetitively will transform that knowledge into wisdom. This is another way to work with the laws of giving and receiving, even in the process of working on any other transformation.

The opposite of this is dabbling, which doesn't give you concrete, lasting results. That's because you're not fact-finding and using your mind as a tool. Instead of trying to master ten things at once (which never works well) choose your priority now so you can be a match to receive the benefits of pursuing it. Although it might seem counterintuitive, you will create more personal balance by picking one thing at a time. And if you need some additional help to focus on that one priority, find a coach, teacher, videos, books, or other resources to stay on target.

Apply the Information You've Gathered—*Helen*

When you successfully use your mind as a tool with principle based thought in giving and receiving, you lay out a strategic, logical plan with a reasonable timeframe, and you'll get a positive result.

Say you want to lose 30 lbs. You're going to have to give yourself a healthier lifestyle to be a vibrational match to receive the weight loss. Obviously, that won't come off in a month. As part of your logical plan, figure out what steps to take to change your eating and exercise habits and how long it will take to weather the plateaus and stay the course on your action plan. Or, if you want to drop judgment or increase forgiveness, you must look at where you are, how much change is necessary to get where you want to go, and what it will take to make it happen.

If you want your business to turn a profit, you need to know that it often takes 3–4 years of giving effort to turn a profit, which means that you might need other sources of income and a plan to become successful, instead of expecting it to happen overnight. What may appear to be an "overnight success" only seems sudden and fast when in truth there are years of choices, perseverance and follow through behind every big success. We often want everything right now; however, there are limits to our energy, so we have to prioritize and be logical about what we give and are likely to receive, so we don't waste time and create lots of disappointment.

To properly apply this information, you must use the Earth-mind as a tool to access Vibrational Law powerfully to have the best experience of you. You must also balance your Earth-mind with your heart-energy. Heart-energy without the Earth-mind being strategic is very messy on our planet, causing negative results like addiction and martyrdom. On the other hand, using the mind without the heart can end up in an abuse of power.

Further Reflection—*Cindy*

"When I talked to Julie," I said, "I did what you're saying. I found someone who was an expert and asked for information so I could stop giving what my friend didn't want."

"How did that go?"

"The next time I saw my friend, I listened and offered support. I did share Linked In strategies with her, but otherwise I stopped trying to get her a job." I hadn't really been happy to stop trying to help. Since I had the new insight that my friend didn't want it, I changed the pattern that had developed in our relationship.

However, I didn't enjoy the friendship as much when my role shifted back to a role of support. While Julie told me that my face means I let people make their own choices and don't try to force things on people, I couldn't bear to see my friend in a painful job search and do nothing but give support. She didn't want to receive what I had to offer, and I didn't want to offer what she was willing to accept. However, we remained friends, and I gave her space.

"Something else happened, too. I stopped feeling like she needed me. Surely that was healthy for both of us," I said.

"When you showed up differently in the relationship and changed the pattern between the two of you, you opened a new possibility," Helen said.

Show Up in the Old Energy Differently—*Helen*

When the universe is trying to give you a message, it happens in correlation and proportion to your expanding desires. When I want to receive something more than what I have, the more I increase my desire, that desire intensifies anything in my energy that doesn't match up because it needs to be processed so I can expand to that new consciousness. For example, if I want to be more patient, I will find myself in even more situations in which I feel impatient and can choose to act patient anyway. That's how I can show up in the old energy of impatience, and practice patience. The more I repeat that pattern, the better I will get at being patient, until I stop trying to be patient, because I already am, and then I'll stop attracting so many opportunities to work on my patience.

When you figure out the energy you want to be in, you're in the energy to receive what you want, and you transform the energy that blocks you. For instance, my cousin was going through a difficult time, and I knew she was in pain, so I invited her to lunch. I told her I could help her come out of the current stress, if she wanted to. She did want relief so I took her through the four questions. She talked it out with me and realized how to align her end in mind in her business and feel centered in that versus attempting to make others happy. After our lunch we ended up getting massages and having the best day.

So, how did I achieve that when the other person was feeling stress? Before I met her, I set my intention to be loving and supportive by her definition, not mine. Why? I get to give love, and that's my agreement I want to expand in. We had a wonderful time, even though it was a hard time for her. With principle-based thought, not only do you often get your target, but you get more. She was vibrating at a much higher frequency when I dropped her off from how she was when I picked her up.

Most people don't know how to do what I did to hold steady and not feed (or entrain to) the pain and stress of others. You want to be the one managing the experience of you, so you need to be crystal clear on your how and why, so you know when you hit the mark. Principle-based thought is how to be consistent.

Post Note—*Helen*

I have saved my thoughts for after you finish learning what's in the next chapter, which continues these ideas about giving and receiving.

CHAPTER 7

PATTERNS OF GIVING AND RECEIVING IN RELATIONSHIPS

The Gift of the Magi—Cindy

I love that it turns out there's a universal law about giving and receiving, because when I have experienced this in my life, I thought it was kind of magical, or maybe I was imagining that things worked this way.

I told Helen I was reminded of the O. Henry story, "The Gift of the Magi," which illustrates what my husband and I went through a lot during our first few years of marriage. The husband and wife want to give each other amazing Christmas presents, so both sacrifice what they love most to buy the other something they will love. In the end, then they both give each other useless gifts. She gives him a chain for his watch, but he sold it to buy her a tortoise clip for her hair, which she sold for his chain.

My husband and I did a similar dance in our early years of marriage. He would ask me what I wanted, and I'd say what I thought he wanted to hear, instead of the truth. We'd try to read each other's minds and drive ourselves crazy trying to make each other happy. That happened with gifts, the bedroom, travel, and even what we wanted for the future.

By the end of the first three years, we'd both had enough and agreed that in the future, we'd stop expecting each other to read minds and ask and tell exactly what we want. This has helped each of us be infinitely happier and more successful in life.

"That's wonderful! Do you know how you worked with the law of giving and receiving to make that agreement work?"

"Not directly, no."

"You took account of your emotional bank account ledgers. Then, you decided what you could and couldn't control about each other's happiness, and you created a ripple effect by working toward outcomes for the highest good," Helen said. I asked her what all that meant, and she gave me the scoop.

Emotional Bank Accounts and How to Give Only What Will Be Received—*Helen*

As Covey puts it, we all have emotional bank accounts, and a deposit from you to someone else isn't registered as a deposit unless it's valued by the person you give it to. If you give something that is of value to you, you might miss the mark if it's not valued by the other person. The key to depositing in emotional bank accounts and building those relationships is learning about each other. You must:

1. Understand the other person.
2. Teach them what's important to you, what makes you feel cared for and what you appreciate.

With my kids, I made deposits in their emotional bank accounts by playing their games and watching their movies. I didn't really like those movies, although I watched them because doing so made my boys happy. On the flipside, with my sons, I had to teach them what made me feel spoiled and appreciated, like saying "please" and "thank you," so they could make those deposits in my account. They made those deposits in my account when they acted with good manners and earned compliments from other people about how well-behaved they were.

For example, one day my son, Sean, was going to an event for the Boy Scouts. He didn't want to wear a jacket because he's very hot-natured, even though it was a cold day. I asked him to at least carry the jacket, to make me look like a better mother, and he agreed to do that for me. It didn't make sense to him to carry the jacket, and because he understood the concept of making deposits in a person's emotional bank account, he did it for me.

Circle of Influence Vs. Energy Drain—*Helen*

Covey defines a circle of concern as including many matters in our lives, such as our health, our children, our work, as well as wider matters like governmental policies, the economy and the environment. A circle of influence includes those concerns that we can actually do something about. That's a very wide range.

To avoid energy drain, *consciously choose* where to spend your time, focus and energy. When I do what fits my personality, meaning things in which I have skills, interests or passions, I can give it 100% because I'm not overextended; I'm not dabbling in things that don't particularly interest me.

Energy drain happens when we agonize over things to which we won't or can't commit sufficient time to cause any meaningful impact. Instead, we diffuse our energy by spending our time and emotions on things that accomplish little or nothing, rather than choosing proactive contribution. We can also experience energy drain by being emotionally reactive instead of being led by principle-based thinking.

We're not here to do everything. We should do what we're called to do and do it well. I wouldn't work on someone's car, because I don't have specialized knowledge of mechanics, so replacing a radiator isn't in my circle of influence. Staying in your chosen circle of influence keeps us from giving aimlessly.

Here are some areas of your life to explore to see if your chosen circle of influence is working with or against your mission:

- If you have a group of friends who make you feel worse, and don't want the same things in life that you want, why would you hang out with them? They're probably influencing you away from the things you want in life, or at the least, probably not helping you evolve toward the experience of your best self.
- Think about marriage. Most people want to marry for love. Along with love, it's important to want the same things long-term as your partner, and for them to share your core beliefs and values. That's a more strategic way to pick someone to love for decades to come.

This comes back to the congruence between givers and receivers and being a match to receive what you want. When I work with clients, I ask them what they want and help them use principle-based thinking and Vibrational Law to get it. Students occasionally get frustrated, because I won't give them my opinion on what to do. I tell them how these laws work so they can see where they're not congruent with what they want. If I did try to give them answers, the results would rarely go the best way, whether the students took the advice or didn't, and that's directly because of the way giving and receiving works. I would be giving too much, out of proportion to my role.

Politics and sports are good examples. Both can be an energy drain when you're worried, complaining, projecting, or debating about things you have no control over. If politics were my circle of influence, I would be very educated in it and taking action, so since I'm not educated in it or active, that indicates to me that politics are outside my circle of influence. If you're not in the circle of influence to affect a particular concern you have, and you're not very passionate about getting in, then that concern is probably not your calling or your business. It's better to use your energy on things you impact and focus your energy there.

Your circle of influence also comes back to clarity. This is the same clarity you use to build a house, have a strong foundation, and make the investment worthwhile. Being successful at anything is about evolving, like the way a marriage evolves. If you marry someone because you feel amazing chemistry, is it logical to assume that you'll stay in that feeling long term? You know that chemistry changes as life, bodies, and circumstances change. My husband and I want to grow old together and raise our children in the same way. We want the same things financially and choose to be in this ever-changing situation. We choose our actions to create our feelings toward and with each other.

As it concerns parenting, I taught my mind to have newer beliefs than the ones I'd previously held from a child's perspective of my experience while growing up. I believe in a loving, good creator, and a divine organization in life, even if I can't see it all the time. I see everything as a gift, invitation, or opportunity to be a better version of myself. If I was always worried about my kids, I would be exhausted. I stay in my circle of influence as a mother and show up and love in a way they can receive. I guide them and set the example as an adult. My circle of influence is my students, clients, family, friends, and everyone who sees my videos or reads my books.

When you act to positively influence your circle, by aligning to your congruent goals, you'll know it's happening. You're being in your business. You'll feel fulfilled, and good things will keep happening. You'll notice that you don't leave other people feeling drained because you didn't entrain down to their vibes. Your relationships will tell you if you're expressing the influence that you want to have. You must watch for signs of progress or stagnation. If you think you're helping someone, and the problem keeps reoccurring, you're not giving them help that they are open to receive; you're enabling them to stay in victim mode. When you use the mind as a tool, everybody benefits, even outside your circle of influence, as you contribute to mass consciousness.

Your positive influence is for people at the right resonance to utilize it. This can sometimes be tough for healers drawn to the metaphysical community to understand what is or isn't their business. You often feel like you can help everyone, and really want to do it. However, if someone you want to help is at a different vibrational level, when you try to help them, it won't be received the way you hoped. If a surgeon is worried about the family's emotions for a patient, that's not a good energy to be in while performing a surgery, because the family's concern isn't in the surgeon's business, it's out of his control. If an energetic healer is determined to make you believe in her work, that's out of congruence with staying in a stable healing vibration that your body can entrain to.

Knowing what is and isn't your business is an excellent way to help others receive benefits, without trying to "fix" them. Others benefit from your high vibrations not only when you're feeling buzzed with positive energy. Even when there's a disappointment, you can use principle-based thinking to give you the best possible experience of yourself and be an uplifting vibration to those in your circle of influence, even in the worst situations or circumstances. Wouldn't you rather be the person who can feel centered and stable, even in situations like a death, natural disaster, etc.? To do so, you'll avoid taking on the worries of others and continue to apply all the principles to get your best outcome, which will encourage others to choose the same.

In Retrospect, It Makes Perfect Sense—*Cindy*

My husband and I moved overseas for his oil and gas job as soon as I finished my Ph.D., so we were thrown into a foreign country at the same time that we started our marriage. We were overwhelmed by figuring out our relationship and negotiating our new social culture, especially his hostile workplace, and the mean-girls group I fell into. We made each other miserable, and were miserable because our energy was being drained, but then we shifted our energy.

"What was the shift?" Helen asked.

"I stopped trying to be friends with everyone, unfriended the women who had harassed me, started being very careful of who I spent my time with," I said. "And, I focused more on 'do I like you,' instead of 'do you like me.' I also read a book about sacred cords and learned that I could protect myself from 'energy vampires.'"

"You know that there's no such thing as an 'energy vampire,' right?"

"What do you mean?"

"There are people who will take your energy if you're willing to give it, and you have a choice. They can't take it if you don't let them."

"That makes sense. I don't know exactly what my husband did, but there were a lot of shake-ups in his company. I kept telling him to keep doing his best work and let the chips fall where they may. He ended up being head-hunted and got his dream job in a company with a much more supportive culture." Today, we make three times the money we made when we were in drama trauma, and we have the time and energy to do animal rescue in addition to being busy with our careers and hobbies.

"When's the last time you had drama with a friend?" Helen asked.

"Not since then. I have even stayed friends with people others have drama with, because that person doesn't do with me what they're supposedly doing with others."

"That's not an accident. You followed principle-based thinking, and I bet your husband did, too."

I thought about it and realized I had done all of Covey's steps:

- I was **proactive** in getting myself out of a toxic environment and into healthier relationships with more centered and grounded people.
- I had the **end in mind** for sure. I didn't want to ever care as much as I did about what others thought of me or waste my time with people who talk about others and judge them, because that's not who I want to be.
- I put **first things first** and stopped accepting that my relationships were "good enough." I made it a priority to drop any relationships that weren't lifting me up, and then only sought out more people like the ones that remained in my new inner circle.
- I went for **win-win** relationships. The girl-drama situation had been lose-lose, and I mean that in a lot of ways. They were always leaving someone out on purpose, and sometimes it was me, but even when I was included, we were losing because we were in the low vibrations of gossip. I changed that energy when I looked for friends that only spoke well of others and themselves, and those were people that could equally give and receive friendship in a win-win.
- **Seek first to understand, then be understood** is how I began evaluating my associations when I considered: "Do I like you?" "Do you make me feel better?" "Am I genuinely interested in you?" Instead of: "Does she like me?"

- **Sharpen the Saw** was also huge for me. I read all kinds of self-help books about toxic friends, and relationships in general. That really helped my marriage, too.
- Finally, in the end I was able to be a match for the higher quality relationships I wanted, both at home with my husband and with my new friends, so I did **synergize**.

I know Helen is so proud of me for finally figuring this out! I am, too.

Create Your Ripple Effect—*Helen*

When you play with the mind as a tool to align with your highest good, it doesn't only affect you. Everyone around you will have a better experience of life, if they choose to be in your circle of influence to receive those positive vibrations. We are influenced by other's actions. If you want to run a 5K, hang out with runners instead of couch potatoes. What you express attracts and repels people to and from your circle of influence. When you choose love over fear, then when people are in your space, they have the invitation to entrain into the best version of themselves.

It's not always easy to keep a higher vibration than others around. And although it isn't your job or business, it is a lovely side effect in that it helps others be the best version of themselves in your space.

CHAPTER 8

THE IMPORTANCE OF BEING IN YOUR BUSINESS

Not Just Minding Your Biz?—Cindy

"You only suffer when you're out of your business," Helen said. A million thoughts popped into my mind. Really? I don't think so. I suffer when I stub my toe, when my husband is traveling for work a lot, and when I have a difficult client. That's my business…I mean, isn't it? I couldn't say that to my client and argue with her, so I chose words to keep the conversation going.

"What does that mean to you?" I asked Helen. She had been saying, "be in your business," all along when we talked about Clarity and Giving and Receiving, and I nodded my head because I thought she meant, "mind your own business." Finally, with this phrase, I realized keeping your eyes on your own paper probably wasn't all she meant. When I thought about minding my own business, I didn't really see how not minding it was the only way I suffer.

She slowed down to really explain what's at stake in being in your business, and how staying in your business can bless you. Helen refers to Byron Katie's *The Work*, which suggests that in this world, there are only three businesses: your business, God's business, and other people's business. God is bankruptcy, flooding, disease, and all the big stuff. In those circumstances, which are beyond your control, how you show up in it and come through it is your business. The harder businesses to sort out are what's your business and what's other people's business. That's why we need Helen and the E's.

Why This Matters—*Helen*

When you enable a problem, by not being in your business, it doesn't change. That's why nagging rarely brings about the desired result. Some people are always talking about other people, conspiracies, and things they have no control over. When you're living your soul purpose, and engaged with your experience of your life, you're controlling how you show up and make an impact. When you simply want other people to think and feel like yourself, that's conditional love, not unconditional love, and that's very painful.

When you're in your business and create a higher vibration, more good reverberates out into the world and you move the needle on the problem. "Be the change you want to see in the world," Gandhi says, and you can cause a ripple effect through mass consciousness. If you think about all the animals you can't save, you will feel bad and help no one. In contrast, if you focus on your rescue pets instead, you are raising the vibe, and that helps more animals and directly helps the ones you serve.

I've been there. There was a time when I wanted to make money to avoid discomfort. I was in a low vibe of wanting to fix things, not in a vibe of happiness, gratitude, and empowerment. Then I realized: as I raise my children to be trustworthy and show up well in life, with intelligence around money and character, that energy ripples out through their friends and interactions. The same ripple is true if they had learned to create suffering, drama and chaos.

In your circle of influence, you make a tangible difference. What's out of your circle of influence is not yours to talk about or stress out about, because you don't want to invest the time to build that influence. Fill your authentic role of yourself, instead of trying to be everything to everyone. The more people who parent well, the more parenting changes.

Your Business Is Where Your Power Is—*Helen*

Your business is where all the power is. Returning to the example of the client who was stuck with a narcissist in her house, when she was reacting to him, there was a lot of darkness, and he did a lot of not-nice things. She had to learn how to build her frequency to a level that was much higher, which would produce a field with which he wasn't a vibrational fit (at an unconscious level). The degree of effort it takes not to react to others, or want them to be different, is at an advanced skill level, and it gets easier the more you practice it. If we wish circumstances, or people, would change, we suffer. And that suffering stems from being in God's or other people's business.

For example, years ago, I asked a psychologist friend who did EFT to help me work through some hurt feelings. I couldn't stop talking about the other person, despite my friend's best efforts to redirect me towards my feelings about the situation. It was so difficult to talk about myself and how I felt. Instead, I was so fixated on this other person and failing to stay in my business, I couldn't focus on my own pain enough to transform it.

You know what that suffering feels and looks like, too, right? No matter what someone else does, if it's not your business, you can't change it or count on it changing. Sometimes you try anyway, which often leads to feeling like you're working hard and not getting anywhere. You feel unappreciated and alone in that struggle.

When it's your business, you are in control. The suffering disappears.

Um, What?!—*Cindy*

Here we were, back to how being in my business would help me suffer less, and as you know, I am very interested in suffering less. Finally, things were making sense. Almost.

"Okay, so when I am suffering," I said, "I can see whether it's my business or not. If it's not, I can stop suffering, AND if it is, I can do something about it, and stop suffering. Is that it?" My mind was exploding. When my husband is traveling and I'm overwhelmed taking care of the house and our pets, whose business is that? The immediate issues of having to do his jobs and mine are my business, or else the trash will never get taken out. But, what about all my feelings about it? All the resentment and loneliness that I blamed on him, whose business was that? Mine or his?

"You're close," Helen replied. "Resisting the reality we find ourselves in does create mental and emotional suffering. Changing our perspective by choosing how we experience ourselves in challenging times creates self-empowerment and vibrational alignment with more of what we would prefer. It isn't the circumstance; it's your thoughts about it that create your emotions." She also reminded me of this quote by Franklin D. Roosevelt:

"Men are not victims of destiny; they are victims of their own minds."

Ouch. That pretty much sums it up. I was suffering when he was gone, although I could stop dwelling on what wasn't my business and stop a lot of it. When his return was delayed, and he couldn't use our opera tickets, I could mope and sigh and suffer. That was my business. Or, I could find a friend to go with me, and find a way to still enjoy the performance. I couldn't change the reality because it was not my business whether his work trip was extended.

Also, accepting a relationship where my spouse frequently travels is my business. So, what was that about? More later.

How to Stay in Your Business—*Helen*

Staying in your business comes back to asking yourself one question: "Is it something you can guarantee solely through your own thoughts, words, and actions?"

If you need someone else to do a certain thing in a certain way, that's not your business. It's difficult because our consciousness in America is to blame other people for what's wrong around us and in others. In that energy, you don't even have enough strength to be in your business and evolve your consciousness. You're too busy spending energy worrying about others. Thus, the more you play with the why and how, the more quickly you can start to see if it's your business or not.

Success isn't measured by whether the other person changes. You know you're staying in your business when you feel great, no matter what they do. Your clarity will help you know what's yours and what isn't. Consistency correlates to the rate of progress, so the more you practice staying in your business, the better at it you will become.

Returning to the client with the narcissist problem, her goal was not to want him back, and she became successful when she didn't want him back because she stopped bouncing back and forth. Getting there was hard, and she had to be willing to walk away from the money and house, and then she attained detachment to when and how he would ultimately leave. I tapped with her and held space for her, yet she was the only one who could create her deep level of unattachment. This kind of unattachment is very advanced clarity and only comes with very hard work.

In my life, I've also had to practice staying in my business. When my sons were on a swim team, we were at a swim team party at a neighborhood pool. A mosquito spray truck went by and sprayed fumes, and I freaked out. I went into victim consciousness and was afraid of getting sick. Then, they drove by and sprayed again! I was so angry and upset, which only hurt me. I was already out of my business, because I couldn't change what happened. I couldn't stop the truck or get the driver fired. It was simply beyond my control.

My son asked me, "Mom, are you being the boss of you?"

I said, "I will be. I need one more minute of complaining." I remembered I could, with effort and focus, release that victim consciousness and come back to what was in my control. I could come back to breathing more good air than bad and was in good health. I could come back to my business.

The only way to evolve yourself out of victim consciousness is to be in your own business. Even if your service is to the world, you can't be attached to how people will receive you or react. Your business is how you show up. That's why, even as a teacher, I can't teach you. You have to teach yourself. My business is how I show up prepared to teach, not how my students respond to or use my teachings.

So, when you need to work on staying in your business in challenging circumstances, there are a few simple things you can do:

- Ask a friend if you're in your business.
- See a coach.
- Write a list of everything you, alone, have the power to change in order to help you analyze what's your business, what's God's, and what's other people's.

Consistency always directly affects the rate of progress, so keep focusing on staying in your business. Sometimes, you might need to lower your emotional charge with EFT so you can engage with the situation productively. That's how I needed to work. I could see that I was in my business when I was being productive. If, on the other hand, I felt stuck in anger, feelings of unfairness or the need to change things outside of my control, then I would use EFT to clear the negative emotion and shift into choosing to be in my own business.

A well-written mission statement can help you anchor in the clarity of what is (or isn't) in your business. Whether you're writing a high-level mission statement for everything in your life, or a more specific mission statement for one of your many identities (parent, spouse, author, etc.), you must be clear (have clarity) whether your target is in your business—achievable solely with your own thoughts, words and actions.

When you have that clarity, you can find yourself again when you're tired, hungry, or stressed out. It's a lifeline when the boat is sinking. When you get tired enough of suffering, you will rediscover what you want and go in that direction. Without that level of clarity and skill of staying in your own business, life will beat you up. As long as you want others or circumstances to change, you will exhaust yourself.

I always said to my kids, you can't possibly get life wrong, although you can always learn to have a much better experience. I never wanted them to feel wrong or be stuck in judgment instead of being solution-oriented, with strong self-esteem and peace of mind.

For my definition of success as a parent, as I mentioned earlier, I had to ask myself with clarity, "How will I know I am successfully raising my kids with good self-esteem?" And the answer was: They will contribute to the world, show up without fear, and be self-motivated. I knew that without these targets, I wouldn't have the clarity to know how to show up as the parent I wanted to be. Note that the choices my children might make as adults is their business, and yet the clarity on my target helped me choose my words, thoughts and actions as a mother. Without clarity on what I was aiming for, I wouldn't have the greatest results, and I would waste a lot of time. The universe does deliver, although to get more of what you want, you need to get busy in your business.

If you're trying to show up in your business, one thing that can trip you up is getting lost in Mass Consciousness, which can amount to not being conscious of the dominant resonance of your vibrations. I've mentioned this term a few times already; Mass Consciousness is the big soup of everyone's thoughts and feelings, and that can mean low- or high-vibes. For instance, today our children have more rights than they did before, and prejudice is evolving out of the mainstream. Health food is also becoming common, and individual doctors are joining in the conversation about holistic medicine. For education, we know now to encourage children and not only punish them. These are ways that mass consciousness on various social and political topics has shifted in my lifetime alone. So, on its own, mass consciousness isn't always bad, although it does need to be evaluated and not taken for granted.

We're always contributing to mass consciousness. It's easy to tap into this shared state to derive creative, useful solutions. Also, unfortunately, on this plane of existence, it's easy to slide into judgment and fearful thinking and contribute to a lower dominant resonance because evolutionarily, that's where we've been. It's harder to move toward love and forgiveness, which shifts mass consciousness to a higher dominant resonance. Either way, I encourage you to be the change you want to see in the world. When you create peace, love, and clarity, you contribute those vibes to the world around you through mass consciousness.

Consider what happens in a mob riot, when some people do things they would never do on their own, because they have defaulted to the influence of the mob consciousness. Yet, there are people who could walk through a mob riot and not even be noticed or touched. Again, that requires the vibrational steadiness of not entraining to the mass consciousness and holding your own self-selected dominant resonance. So, when you purposefully stand in clarity and choice, you separate from the vibration of mass consciousness by being instead in your business. In this country, habitual stress is a common denominator in mass consciousness; it's accepted because stress can even be a bragging right and an expected part of success. If you don't have stress, what else might you have? I prefer inner peace and positive expectation, both of which increase efficiency and effectiveness. End in mind, anyone?

Post Note—*Helen*

I put together a few final thoughts on this subject, each with an example to help you quickly apply the lesson. Enjoy!

- Without the understanding of being in your business, the principles can't work at all!

Examples: *Being in a contest and setting your goal to win means stress and pain, because you aren't the judge. Paying to produce a book, for the intention of making financial profit, leaves you at the mercy of people you do not know how to reach or consistently influence. Not having a personal definition of a "good" mother leaves you without guidance when triggered emotionally.*

- Having an end in mind of changing others and being in their business is always a painful goal.

Examples: *If the goal is winning a contest, we have no control over the judges' opinions or the quality of other contestants' entries. Wanting to control your adult children is fruitless because they are living their own unique lives in a radically different era than the one you grew up in.*

- There is no "proactivity" in desiring to change, fix, heal, or control others—it all comes from fear and creates pain for many.

Examples: *Needing to win means that losing hurts. Needing book sales means you are at the mercy of forces you can't count on. Needing your sons to think like you, be like you, is insanity, since they are not you and don't have your specific chemistry, emotions, memories, or identity.*

- No one truly wins over time when change is not authentic or aligned to truth. Choice and acceptance—not force— empower us. Even the controller will not have happiness when others acquiesce out of fear.

Examples: *Winning is the vibration of success—hating 'winners' means you are aligning to the opposite vibes! Being in the negative energies of losing for prolonged periods only limits the future potential of becoming masterful and creates a personal loss for all who would be a part of continuous growth, such as: judges, marketers, publishers, writers, readers, Amazon, etc.*

- There is no "first things first" that will bless you, if you aren't in your business and in a higher vibe. Feeling victimized doesn't create what you want, ever!

Example: *Wanting to change what is, in reality, by force only creates more vibrational alignment to what you don't want, "what you resist persists." "As within so without," is a common adage meaning that, if you are in frustration over others or situations, you align to more frustration.*

- If you're busy wanting to change others you can't possibly understand their experience, consciousness, or the gift of their uniqueness.

Examples: *Never relating to the love of competition or contests means you'll drop out before finding what you're capable of. Needing a first book to be a bestseller means you'll stop or doubt yourself and the value of what you offer—even though those close to you give endless testimony of the value of your work. Expecting "mini-me's" out of your children means you miss the gift of who they are!*

- You aren't learning anything new if you think you know it all! If you believe that your way is the only way that is right, you won't seek new information. Nothing new will evolve if you only interact with others of like minds.

Examples: *A blog spewing the unfairness of losing never creates winners. Blabbing about all the hardships of getting a book out never creates positive buzz around the book. Not learning how to love your children in thought, action, and word means you repeat the conditional love other parents have expressed.*

Can you see how each principle naturally overlaps to include them all for a successful experience?

CHAPTER 9

BE YOUR DOMINANT RESONANCE INTENTIONALLY

Unintentional Dominant Resonance—Cindy

One thing that has always bugged me about the whole Law of Attraction is competition. If there are 50 children in the spelling bee, they all want to win, but only one will. I tend to lose competitions, and it really bothers me, because I am otherwise a very successful person. The only time I lose is when I enter a bonafide contest. It's uncanny. It started with a public speaking contest when I was a child. After the same boy beat me three years in a row, I chose to stop competing, lest I get beaten again.

I asked Helen, "What about the things you want that are just not for you? When do you give up?"

"You create your perception of reality, and still, you don't one-up God," she began. Well, that made sense. If something qualifies as a natural disaster, that's not about one person's intention to live in a safe place. However, that wasn't what I meant exactly, so I tried again.

"Okay, and what about when you put in the time to practice and learned what you needed to, and you participated with an anticipation to win, and you still lose?" I asked.

She clarified that you can't grow wings, although you can create your perspective. In this case, I was letting myself be victimized by the pain of defeat—that's a choice. I could've also had gratitude for the way I was leveling through the challenge of not being the winner today, with positive expectations. The latter is not what I chose the first time I lost. As a result, I was motivated by regret, frustration, and disappointment. Those feelings created my perception of myself in reality, and that was the energy I unintentionally showed up in.

I remember after the third loss, the mother of the boy who kept winning came and talked to me. I didn't cry at the event, but I'm sure I looked like I was about to. She told me I had done a good job, and not to give up on myself. I have never forgotten that kindness, yet it wasn't enough for me to compete again. I still wouldn't dare to dream of joining Toastmasters. I am a great public speaker, and am often invited to give talks and presentations. My poor soul couldn't bear to be scored against others in that scenario.

However, Helen showed me that maybe I could. I could set my intention for a higher energetic resonance. Instead of having low-vibes while I practice and prepare my speech, I can be in high-vibes. Once that higher vibration is dominant, you don't have to pay attention to it anymore, the way riding a bike becomes second nature, Helen explained. This chapter breaks down how you can set your dominant resonance by choice and practice it consistently. If you've been losing at what you want, keep reading.

The Breakdown on Dominant Resonance—*Helen*

Your dominant resonance is diverse and complex, and it includes what thoughts others project onto you, as well as your habitual patterns of thought and action. This cohesive resonance includes genetics, mass consciousness, biology, physiology, personality, soul agenda, environment, and more influences in your energetic field. In keeping with the radio metaphor, while we all bounce up and down the dial every day for the most part, your dominant resonance is the higher or lower vibrational channel where you show up most frequently.

In any one moment, there are different layers and levels of vibration, and we don't yet even know them all. Once you do a lot of work to transform unresolved pain, judgment and limitation from all the bodies (see Chapters 15 and 16), etc., then you want to watch out because you begin creating your experience very quickly. You can slip into old victim consciousness thoughts and suddenly trip, or spill coffee! For me it's a great reminder to choose my thoughts in that moment. (Previously the patterns were so old and stagnant I couldn't recognize what preempted what I was experiencing.) You can attract amazingly wonderful things that stretch your comfort zone emotionally and energetically while staying conscious and consistent in yes-energy.

Even though we might be in the same space at the same time with someone else, we can be having very different experiences, filtered through each person's perceptions and dominant resonance. It's like reading a book, something different stands out to you than another reader, because you are coming from a different place. Or, when a speaker speaks, the listeners each pick up something slightly different from their understanding of the speaker's tone or inflection.

Your diverse experience of life on Earth goes through all your filters and perceptions to form patterns. The more you repeat a pattern, the more dominant that pattern's vibration becomes in your resonance. Look at things about yourself and your life that you wish were other than they are. Then, look at the common beliefs that surround those things. Should you believe it? If you have a pattern that's not attracting to you more of what you want, maybe it's time to change the vibration. For instance, why do I have a round belly? Why am I aging into an apple shaped body rather than a slim or pear-shaped body? Why do I believe I shouldn't, or should? Because it's in my family as a genetic coding from my grandmother and mother, so, to flatten my tummy or lose abdominal fat, I change my consciousness about what's normal for my body.

Your rate of consistency equals your rate of progress, as I mentioned earlier. So, when you want to change a pattern to change the vibration, the more you repeat the new pattern, the more quickly you tap into the higher vibration. For example, if a person talks about how money multiplies, and is of service, they grow money; when people talk about how awful money is and how hard it is to manage, they attract those problems for themselves. As you understand how this plays out, you can influence your experiences by being in your business. Accidents, disease, war—these things do happen outside our circle of influence, and still, the control you have is choosing how you show up in that situation. As Bob Riley states, "Hard times don't create heroes. It is during the hard times when the 'hero' within us is revealed."

To reveal my hero within, I created my personal mission statement for life, which is: "I am a catalyst for positive change." I always purposefully align to my intention in any situation in a way that serves my mission statement. Ask anyone I've ever worked with. I can always find the positive in any circumstance; therefore, more positivity flows through me for me, by me, and with me. I have an amazing life. It's because I am an excellent storyteller, and I can turn any set of events around into a great story that benefits me.

Choose Your Dominant Energy, and Practice It Consistently—*Helen*

When you're harmonious with what you want in your thoughts, speech, and actions, and aligned with your identity, mission statement, end in mind, and goal, you are choosing your dominant energy. A good example of an intentional dominant resonance is Cesar Milan, who doesn't react with anger or fear with the dogs he trains, no matter how aggressively they behave at times. He holds steady with the formula that works; eventually the dogs will change, and he will achieve his goal. This is principle-based thinking, followed through with consistent action, and these Spiritual Laws are about how to think and improve your life both personally and professionally.

Think about two very different feelings, faith and fear. Did you know that they are both the same vibration? They're both projections of expectation. Faith is the belief in what you don't yet see evidence, while fear is the belief in something you don't want that you don't yet see any evidence. If your dominant energy is expectation, be aware of whether you are projecting that with fear or faith.

If you focus on fear, you get more fear until you focus on courage.

With this book, and as a teacher, I am very congruent with my overall life mission of being a catalyst for positive change. So, I'm committed to maintaining a steady high vibration so that others can listen and feel supported. I have built that skill over time. I keep talking about my book, and am working on my thoughts, words, and actions to feel good about its creation. I can be in faith that this book will be successful and be read and shared by many people who will go into action, or I can be in fear that the book will be hard to market. If I remain in fear, people will reflect back that energy and be worried for me and tell me stories of failures. If I remain in faith, people will tell me about others who are successful authors. I get to choose how I set my expectation, and either way, I'm going to get it. That's how it works.

"If you think you will or think you won't, either way, you're right." Zig Ziglar.

Whatever dominant energy you wish to assume, you must ask yourself, "am I being consistent?" You're using the mind with logic and strategy to stay focused on what you want, aligned through your thoughts, words, and action no matter what else is going on. To have the best experience, you must be congruent with how you want to experience yourself and life. A great athlete is always learning and practicing their skill set and sport. They immerse themselves to be successful. Someone who's great with money can talk about it for hours without getting tired of it. When you start something new and want to reach that level, you must practice.

Hold Up—*Cindy*

I started to feel frustrated again when Helen was talking about practice. After all, I had practiced my speeches for hours at a time. I recited them in front of a mirror, outside while addressing the cows in our barn, and I didn't start over when I mixed up a word, but always kept going and finished each round. My problem was not consistency. So, I challenged her.

"Sometimes when you are consistent, and you do practice, you don't win. Think about Olympic athletes." She conceded that someone with a better build for a sport might have a little help from God in their DNA, and yet I still wasn't satisfied.

I hate to talk about myself with a client, yet there I was doing it again. I reminded her that I'd said earlier I had practiced a lot. I have made peace with those losses in the past by reminding myself that the boy had a speech writer and coach, and I didn't, so it wasn't a level playing field. I mentioned that to Helen, and she saw something else.

"Yes, Cindy, you were in right action, yet you didn't keep creating the pattern. After three tries, you quit. How many tries does an Olympic athlete make?" I got her point.

I had lacked the resilience to keep trying to create the pattern I wanted in the face of not getting it. The video playing in my mind was the one when I tried my hardest and it wasn't good enough. And, as we established earlier in this chapter, my dominant resonance had been awash with no-energy, even though I had been taking the right steps.

Let's Review with a Few Examples—*Helen*

Someone who's successful in business and enjoys a steady flow of wealth might spend only 1–2% of their energy understanding the problem and then 98% of their energy working on the solution. In this way, they attract solutions and repel problems. For most of us, we're mesmerized by problems, yet we could be mesmerized by solutions to be more successful. If you want patience, you are going to have lots of opportunities to practice patience—when circumstances triggering impatience show up—until the new habit is formed. You keep learning until you master it.

If you're a parent, you know what it's like to want to hurt a child when you're tired. Yet, you wouldn't hit or hurt them, because that's not who you want to be. So, you focus on how to contain that urge and dismiss it. When you're stretching into a new level of accomplishment or consciousness, you want to be able to do the same thing. The more clarity you have and knowledge of how to achieve your goal, the more the influences around you will match and support your energy.

At first, old patterns will present themselves as enticing opportunities to be reactive and fall back on your old ways. Clarity, consistency, belief, and action comprise the pattern to get what you want or don't want. You're using the pattern without being aware of it, and becoming aware of it enables you to use it strategically for yourself.

Failing to become the dominant energy you want looks like morphing into a copy of whomever you're with. You won't be able to hold steady with thoughts, words, and actions to get you what you want, because it's not coming from an authentic place. And that's because you're in a generational pattern that's much bigger than you, or you're retreating to an old pattern you learned before. With awareness, you can re-align yourself with a higher vibration and reset your dominant resonance to be where you want it.

Post Note—*Helen*

I saved my thoughts for after you finish learning what's in the next chapter that continues these ideas about your dominant resonance.

CHAPTER 10

HOW TO BE YOUR DOMINANT ENERGY INTENTIONALLY

You Always Have a Dominant Resonance, and You Can Always Choose It—Cindy

I realized that when I didn't get what I wanted, like losing the speaking contests, I would only see what I didn't get and be washed over with low vibrational feelings and limiting beliefs that would drag me further down. I didn't see the good: I was learning a skill that would serve me well into adulthood; my hunger to be better at speaking would send me all the way to a minor in communications, and a speech writing and analysis class in which I would make an "A"; and one day, I would be a paid speaker. I didn't get the blue ribbon that day, yet in life, I won really big, because I participated.

I don't like to dwell on what might've been, but I do wonder. Seeing that I still benefited and had an overall good outcome from the speaking contest, because of my practice and learning, how much better might so many other things have been for me if I had not succumbed to feeling like a loser? And at this point, I asked Helen, "When I am in a losing position now, how do I do something different than I have in the past?"

"It's not going to be easy, and you can change your dominant resonance around competition and losing," she said.

I gave it some thought. I can control whether, how much, and how well I practice and learn new information, although I can't make a judge pick me. That's not my business, as we discussed previously. I started wondering if I could feel so much like a winner that I could have all the feelings and positive self-talk I would expect to have when I won, even if I lost? It felt like a stretch, yet it also started to seem possible within Helen's paradigm.

Five Ways to Raise Your Dominant Energy—*Helen*

Creating a new dominant resonance means you have to get the information, use the mind as a tool to understand the end in mind, utilize principle-based thoughts, and practice acting in accordance with those parameters. To do this, you can:

- Hold your energy congruent with the dominant resonance you want. Be really present, which is a skill you have to build stamina for. You know best what thoughts, words, and actions comport with the identity you want to hold.
- Ask good questions, have clarity, and define what you want.
- Use Law of Attraction language to achieve your energy. If you speak in scarcity and need, you will receive more of that. In contrast, if you speak in goodness and gratitude, you receive more things for which to be grateful.
- Read Covey's book once a year for five years in a row to truly understand principle-based thinking.

When I show up as a student, my dominant energy is organized, prepared, and confident. If I were jumping all over the place or forgetting what I asked or didn't take notes, that wouldn't feel very good.

Know that your energy is your responsibility. For empaths who say things like others "drain their energy," or insist they are "sensitive to loud noises or certain energies," then their field is too open, and they can learn to manage their sensitivities to benefit themselves.

You must learn about your energy field and accept responsibility for it. Also, all your emotions are yours, and they can be great gifts and messengers. No one makes you feel anything.

With relatives during the holidays, you might become triggered and really want to go into an old pattern. By being aware of that possibility, you can develop a strategy, practice in your mind, and get a coach or do the spiritual work to break that pattern to give you the result you prefer. Similar to how you take your car to a mechanic when there's a problem, if you have a problem getting triggered, you may benefit from a coach, therapist, or spiritual leader to support you with the right tools to transform the energy patterns that trigger you. Always know you want to use the mind as a tool. Utilize your mind to serve your higher self, through focus and intention with choosing the thoughts you think.

"The mind is a great servant, but not a great master." Robin Sharma

By the same token, you're not responsible for the reactions of others, so long as you run your thoughts, words and actions through the filters of thoughtfulness and respect. If someone is being reactive, what's your skill set in understanding? If someone is in a reactive mode, they're not using their mind intelligently. They are running on emotions that are repressed, or on beliefs and action that are from mass consciousness or inherited—you don't have access to those unless the person verbalizes them. If you understand what emotions mean energetically, you will have the right response to help them process what they are feeling.

Vibrationally, when you choose to align your thoughts, words, and actions to the highest outcome, you give yourself the resonance to attract your same emotional vibration. Committing to learning, practicing, and choosing a vibration of love and intelligence will vibrationally keep reactive people out of your circle. They'll sense that their vibrational resonance isn't a fit with yours, even if they aren't aware of it.

Recognize Your Dominant Energy—*Helen*

You will know what your dominant frequency is by looking at your relationships. What's reflected back to you the most? Do Louise Hay's exercise for attracting wealth. She suggests that you look at your closest 5–10 friends on matters of money—that's what your money-vibration is. If you don't like it, then learn how to change it. I know people in all kinds of income brackets today. Money is easy today, after years of work. Your beliefs aren't hidden, like a fish in water who doesn't know it's in water. Whatever is around you is showing up because of your vibration.

When something you want is not yet your dominant resonance, you haven't picked or aligned to what you want long enough for it to become dominant. Any pattern of emotion, thought, or physical structure takes a lot of action to undo. Look at how long the old pattern has existed. Is it in your family line or mass consciousness? You could drop dead, and the pattern would still exist. That takes a lot of effort to change. For example, there was so much anger in my family line. Even my son came into the world angry. I worked on transforming that pattern of anger, and now I can't tell you the last time someone around me was angry. When I was holding the resonance of anger, I could see people arguing across a room, and I would feel anger. Today, I don't have that experience.

Logically, what you choose to surround yourself with impacts your dominant energy. When you surround yourself with something, you get into alignment with its pattern. So, you can pick things to align with. Laughter is contagious, and so is anger. If you watch enough funny videos, you will find humor everywhere; if you listen to enough angry politics, you will get angry about politics.

Be sure your dominant energy is not hampered by desires to "fix others." When you're in a level of clarity in your own business, you aren't trying to fix, save, or heal anyone else. You're withdrawing the energy of projecting others in the role of the victim, which gives them the choice to accept help or not. Thinking you have to be the savior is a belief system that others need to be saved. That belief system actually undermines your goal of helping others, because they will entrain to be the victim, and they won't be receptive to your help. They might even become angry with you. Offering help from compassion instead of pity means others can feel supported. The pattern of co-dependence will repeat, until you start speaking and acting differently—until you are no longer a match for those relationships and aren't reacting to drama and trauma.

You are a diverse being in many different realities and energies. When you've mastered the energy to be congruent with your goals, you will achieve your results, if not in physical form, then in your feelings, no matter the result. What I mean is that if you don't get exactly what you wanted, you will feel the way you'd wanted to feel and may even end up with something better than you had intended.

Putting It Together—*Cindy*

I felt like I was getting some things right when I took a look at my life. I have some clients with 8- and 9-figure businesses; surely, they wouldn't have been attracted to work with me if I had a lot of toxic baggage. At the same time, I know my rates aren't nearly as high as they should be, and the only reason they are low is that I set them there. There's something about the value I see in myself that's lacking. Other people see my value, though. I don't have an image problem, but rather a self-perception problem.

That all stems from feeling like a loser as a little girl, and I'm sure that there are ways I protect myself from further losing by not ever entering competitions. So, I entered a competition inside the Copy Chief membership site for professional writers. I couldn't believe that I was doing it, and still, I participated, consciously trying to change my dominant resonance. I blessed the other entries and sent them positive thoughts. I created my entry with a sense of joy and confidence, and I submitted it with the absolute expectation that I will blow them out of the water. Then, I entered, the hard part for me. I had to keep my vibration high and not allow all those feelings from the past losses to resurface—and keep my vibration high even if I lost. I understood how that would work, but I wasn't sure if I could handle choosing a high vibration in an emotional situation, so Helen gave me a strategy to play with so I could practice.

Start Playing with Energy Dominance—*Helen*

Take a look at your life. What energies are dominant? Is there a lot of laughter, optimism, and love, or is there a lot of worry, stress, and loss? Your energy field is a reflection of your consciousness. How are you experiencing money, creativity, ease, flow, and time? Whatever your answer is, that's how you're interacting with the matrix of everything and the dominance of the energy most potent in your field.

Finding my dominant resonance and raising it, if it's a low vibe, is a skill I developed with practice. I was always afraid about money, even about Christmas gifts. After I saw *The Secret*, I was captivated by the scene with the woman putting the bill in the mailbox, and there's all this worry energy coming off of her. My field was also one of fear, which is vibrationally in alignment with scarcity and stress, so the fear and stress I was vibrating kept attracting more of that to me.

Raising your vibrations is especially tricky in the Physical Body, because it's hard to be in the resonance of health when your body gives you messages of not-health. You use all the energy bodies to see and remember all the health you have in your body and what is working. You can then focus, feel, and speak of health and align your consciousness to the consciousness of health.

For example, if someone is a hoarder or has chronic clutter, the Law of Attraction limits flow and growth. In that case, the stagnant energy in their home is a stronger resonance than they are, and it's very painful for them to change. Excessively holding on to things is often about unresolved grief. A friend of mine discovered this for herself in cleaning out her mother's house. She has boxes she feels unable to get rid of because doing so will feel like releasing her grief, and she's not ready. Grief is dominant for her now. As she heals, she can choose gratitude instead, and then her dominant energy will change.

Whatever your dominant energy is now, know that change is possible and doable. Reflect on where your vibrational frequency is now, and if something feels less than positive or joyous, consider a few questions:

- What's your consciousness in that moment?
- What are you thinking?
- What are you feeling?
- What belief system is at play?
- What's your physical reaction/where do you feel this in your body?

Practice scanning your energy to determine your dominant energy when you feel good, so you can be aware of how to think and feel in order to get back to that mentality when you don't feel so wonderful. The next time life happens, and you feel yourself getting dragged into an old pattern that doesn't serve you, run through this energy scan to identify where your resonance is off-track. You can quickly reset your dominant resonance, first through thought and then action, to a higher vibration that will help you get your best possible outcome. The habit of principle-based thought creates a dominant resonance.

Dabbling creates more inconsistent dabbling, until you focus on stamina-building.

Post Notes—*Helen*

Thinking about your dominant resonance brings you into self-observation and exploration to discover beliefs, thoughts, words and actions that do not match the principle-based thoughts that align you to what you desire next in life. Everything that you already have, 'good' or 'bad', means you are aligned to the end result through your beliefs, focus, habits, expectations, and actions. Many beliefs are inherited and run behind the scenes until we begin to **seek to understand ourselves**.

Here's a run-down on principle-based thought for creating a high dominant resonance:

End in mind: Choose resonance that is consistently a match to your definition of good, happiness, health, and ease. Once this is your target, you can reset yourself when coasting towards victim consciousness or suffering.

Examples: *Feeling like a successful author on the journey to success, by my standard.*

Proactive: Purposefully choose to be in higher vibes through perspective, thoughts, words and actions. Choose the response in any situation that is a match vibrationally to what you desire.

Examples: *Acting and feeling like a winner (a successful author) no matter what, until that becomes my one dominant feeling, which aligns me to more success.*

Win/win/win: I prefer a dominant resonance that addresses these three wins:

1. When you live in harmony with love and ease your life works well.
2. Others in your life have a better experience with you.
3. You bless our world through choice and consciousness of more and more good.

Examples:

1. *Finding writing a fulfilling experience.* **AND** *I have a joyous experience working with Cindy.*
2. *I bless the contests that bring many writers and readers together.* **AND** *Cindy, in turn, benefits as she applies the teachings.*
3. *This allows more contests and more winners to be created in the future.* **AND** *Cindy, the publisher, sellers, and readers profit in various ways; at the same time, I profit through producing more books to bless more lives.*

First things first: Research (learn) what thoughts and feelings carry higher vibes so you can be in choice to shift into them as a dominant resonance instead of fear (the base of all negative emotions).

Examples: *What does success feel like? What does it feel like to hear that your book helped someone with a problem or changed their life for the positive? Feeling gratitude to share written work and gratitude for all the people, publishers, contests, blogs etc. that make it possible to connect readers to writers.*

Seek to understand: What is my current dominant resonance, and what is the dominant resonance I want to achieve? What is my business—what exactly do I control in sharing through written word? Why am I writing? Who will benefit? What energy is behind my writing and my desires? What is normal in our culture today for contests and first-time published books? How do I love the action of what I'm choosing, and at the same time love myself no matter the financial benefit or reaction to what I've produced? What are the 'hows' and 'whens' that are definitely not in my control? How does this bless my life?

Examples: *Contests pick a limited number of winners. There are only certain people interested in what I am interested in writing. The opportunity to share is the energy that fulfills me. One reader that benefits from my writing means I am doubly blessed. I can't create overnight success that lasts (by financial measure in our world today) without years of consistent action, and consistent positive expectation in those years.*

Sharpen the saw: Choose to continuously learn to deepen understanding and become masterful in any chosen endeavor.

Examples: *Sharpening the saw toward writing contests by taking positive actions of exploring available contests and their associated topics, genres, rules and eligibility requirements. Right action of learning about publishing, marketing and what readers want and need can sharpen the saw to get a book to more people who would benefit.*

Synergy: Focusing on the potential extra benefits created when separate beings work together expands the dominant resonance of connection, expansion and abundance through giving and receiving.

Examples: *Contests can't exist without submissions, promotions, entry fees, judges, and prizes. A book benefiting others can't exist without a writer, information, publication, sellers, and readers.*

Can you see how each principle naturally overlaps to include them all to create a dominant resonance for a successful experience?

CHAPTER 11

THE FOUR-PART FORMULA TO CREATE CONSCIOUSLY

Some of My Previous Ideas About Manifesting Were Just Wrong—Cindy

You might've noticed that Helen manages to talk about the Law of Attraction without ever saying "manifest." At first it was so hard for me to even program my brain to think that way that I plugged in my word when she described what she calls "conscious creation." After the first draft of the book, she brought up this point, and I was speechless.

I offered to change it since I'd used a word she wouldn't, and that would be an easy "Find and Replace" edit to get my words out. More importantly, we realized there was more I just wasn't getting about what makes Helen's unique take on this different from what I've heard before.

"Okay," I began, "I want to understand what you said. Isn't the whole point of the Law of Attraction to manifest what you want? Isn't that why you need clarity?"

"Partially, yes. As we discussed earlier, you need clarity so you only ask for your best outcome, and you're consciously creating your best outcome, not 'manifesting.'"

I tried to process this new information as best I could. I had always thought I was manifesting clients, opportunities, and even things I didn't want, like traffic jams or my back problems. Wasn't that how it works? I wondered if we were splitting hairs over the same basic concept, so I gave it another shot. "Why 'conscious creation' instead of 'manifesting?' I thought I was using the Law of Attraction to bring into reality what I want."

"You are. What's different about my angle is that you're working with the universe on multiple levels. You're not holed up in your bedroom with a vision board and thinking that will get you to a penthouse in Hawaii. You're consciously co-creating your reality. And, with my system, which includes using logic for personal growth, you can be intentional and use your mind to create the highest good and best outcome for yourself, your circle of influence, and the planet."

The light started to go on in my mind. She reminded me that she'd said that the formula to consciously create any outcome is the same on Earth for everything and includes: Clarity, Consistency, Belief, and Action.

"The 'conscious' part means being awake," she explained, "and not running your thoughts on autopilot in mass consciousness. And there's a lot more to it. You have to be highly self-aware, see yourself honestly, and understand your feelings in order to have the consciousness necessary to do this work of consciously creating on purpose with purpose."[14]

She was right. If I want something, I don't merely add it to my vision board and write gratitude affirmations about it. I get into action and realize that if I'm not motivated to action, there's probably something out of alignment between me and the goal.

---

[14] Breaking down that phrase to its component parts: On purpose means intentionally, and with purpose means with alignment to your underlying mission or purpose.

Strengthen Your Consciousness by Acknowledging the Obstacles in Your Life—*Helen*

Patterns will always repeat on this plane of existence until you bring consciousness to them. That consciousness applies the four parts of conscious creation: Clarity, Consistency, Belief, and Action. For instance, when you build a restaurant, there are a lot of moving parts before everything is in place to serve food to people. You need **clarity** about so many things, from the menu to the décor and target clientele; you have to work **consistently** to market yourself, develop recipes that always come out the same, **believe** that your restaurant is amazing and worth all your effort, and stay in **action** to help it be successful. It's the same with building mental consciousness. You are putting all these new chosen moving parts into the existing pattern to change it or replace it.

Say you want to be less judgmental. You can't decide on a whim not to be judgmental or be resistant to the judgment. You can't make yourself wrong for being judgmental; that's only adding more judgment to the judgment. When those thoughts come up, acknowledge what's happening for clarity. If you consistently choose to replace judgmental thoughts with higher vibrational thoughts (such as gratitude) and believe the change is possible, you will eventually rewire your brain to go straight to those positive thoughts.

To be in a new consciousness, you're transforming a pattern or belief system that you inherited or co-created. To transform energy, you have to show up in the old energy and do something different to stop pushing and resisting. For example, if you want to increase your wealth, and you don't have experience with handling large amounts of money, then change your energy field to expand to that skillset. To be a match for a lot of money to come in, first gain an understanding of money and how it works in the current culture. Gain an understanding of how money can be budgeted, managed and grown. Then work on any self-worth issues, limiting beliefs, or negative judgments about wealthy people. That's the clarity piece. With that clarity, you'll be able to consistently practice the habits of wealthy people through the way you think, speak, and take action, which eventually has you 'feeling' wealthy. At that point, you're in the new belief of wealth as normal, and it must show up around you when all these pieces are in in vibrational alignment!

My brother didn't have a consciousness for ease with money. So, when he wanted to increase his wealth, I suggested that he increase his understanding of managing money by getting knowledgeable about money terms and concepts through books. Without using the mind as a tool, you don't have space for a new identity when you want to create one for yourself. So, if you get a bonus, or inherit money, and then it goes out the door immediately, consider the possibility that you weren't yet a conscious vibrational match for keeping and building wealth.

As another example, if I want to consciously create a loving relationship with my mother, I shift into an energy of love for her ability to rock and roll in her reality, which is quite different from mine. In action, I meet her in love, stop speaking in judgment, change my body language, and then I ask myself, "how can I see my mother in a way that I can feel true love?" I have clarity that there are ways she didn't receive unconditional love and didn't know how to give it. As a result, she was unable to give me the childhood I wanted, and I will never get that from her. Now, I don't need her to give it to me, so I shift my belief about the relationship, allowing me to choose to let unconditional love flow through me to her, which I practice consistently.

This work took years, because I wasn't merely overcoming our mother-daughter pattern; I overcame similar mother-daughter patterns in mass consciousness as well. Think about how strong such old, harmful patterns can be. If a 5-year-old loses a parent, the energy of loss and grief will arise at every big stage of consciousness:

as a teen, getting married, having children, etc. And, that is an invitation to transform the old energy of loss and grief at different stages of consciousness.

How Is This Working for Me?—*Cindy*

"I've got a difficult relationship with someone from my past. She's very controlling, and I'm trying to change the dynamic between us. Can I tell you a quick story?" I asked. Helen nodded. I told her that person sent me an email, basically giving me an emotional guilt trip to travel to her, and when that happened, I tried to do something differently than I would in the past in order to get a different result. So, I sent a polite email declining to attend and wished her well with what she was working on.

"It worked, kind of," I said, "because I'm not going, and I didn't let her win, but she sent me this pain in my neck." My stress about this person is a literal pain in my neck.

"Your friend didn't make your neck hurt," Helen replied.

"Yes, she did. She doesn't do it consciously, and when she's controlling, that message sends me physical pain."

"That can only happen if your field is open to her control giving you neck pain," Helen said gently.

"But I did show up in the old energy and chose something different. I didn't let her control me."

"You weren't open to being controlled, and you replied with love and gratitude, and that action is going to bless you both. If you want to add not getting neck pain when, and if, she tried to be controlling again, you can choose that, too. That's about being very self-aware and intentional."

I thought back to how I had noticed in other situations that I create my back pain. This explained how it all worked.

Strengthen Your Consciousness by Cultivating Intentionality—*Helen*

If your project is for you to be more conscious and intentional, you must know your 'what,' 'why,' 'how,' and 'how you know you're successful' to keep yourself on track. To help my students with this challenge, I send them a daily text with a statement and a question to both engage them and help them show up consciously. Another great tool to help you show up consciously is the Meaning to Pause® bracelet, which has a vibration that goes off in specific intervals to remind you to regularly be grounded or anchored in gratitude. You are the one to set up tools and implement a strategy. You can treat your spiritual growth the same way you treat planning a wedding, building a business, or buying a car. There's a certain protocol with all of these tasks, and your spiritual growth is the same. You have to be logical about your personal growth the same as anything else.

Employing Self-Awareness—*Helen*

Self-awareness means you can recognize and name the patterns, as well as understand the complexity of yourself, which is a big part of the clarity piece of conscious creation. Hopefully, you want to be self-aware in love, instead of in victim consciousness and saying, "I am this way because of my parents, the government, etc." It's also asking yourself, "what makes me tick?"

"Life isn't about finding yourself. Life is about creating yourself."— George Bernard Shaw

I'm more self-aware today than I was 5 years ago because I'm engaged in a daily relationship with myself instead of always being in other people's business or focusing on why things aren't working. Now

I spend time with myself. I spend time writing my 10 gratitude statements and why I'm grateful for them (thank you Rhonda Byrne for your book, *The Magic!*). I had to develop my profound self-awareness journey to get to this point, and I will keep developing it. I'm self-aware each time I stay focused on my mission statements for each of my identities (parent, author, spouse, etc.) and how I show up in each role. Your self-awareness literally grows in proportion to your skill in making choices.

Another important self-awareness tool is to work on your authenticity. No one can tell you what to think or give you the answer, so you have to be honest with yourself about what you think, which is where you will also find your core beliefs. That basic integrity within yourself will build your authenticity. Create a relationship with yourself instead of becoming a carbon copy of a mentor or guru. Honor the Divine by being the best version of your authentic self. You want to evolve in goodness in your unique self by speaking honestly when benefit can be created.

Inauthenticity is running patterns based on habit or fear, so no wonder that people love authenticity. When I own up to my struggles and strengths, I own everything, and I am authentic. If I say I am a guru and always perfect, I am not authentic. If I bring up the past when nothing can be changed, I'm cruel, not honest. If you're not choosing conscious authenticity, you're limiting the good that can come through you and to you from others. Inauthenticity means there's something about yourself you don't accept, or think is wrong, or you are worried about how others will perceive you.

Authenticity is yes-energy calmly saying, "Yes, yes I am everything—creative and kind-hearted, but also lazy and stingy at times." Inauthenticity is no-energy nervously claiming, "I can't face that," and, "I can't let you see that." I don't have to agree with my mother's choices in life or her belief system or how she shows up, and I can still enjoy loving her and be authentic. The authenticity is that I don't agree with her, and I am in choice, and I choose love without agreeing or condoning everything about her.

Consistently practice both empathy for others and self-empathy. As far as emotions go, if you can understand it, you can utilize it. All emotions exist to motivate a response. Each energy is part of our guidance system. You're hard-wired to feel emotions before thought, so it's important to understand the logic of how they work so you can skillfully utilize them. If your Emotional Body is very wounded, you have a backlog of emotions. And when your Emotional Body is backlogged, you can get so angry you can't speak, freeze when you should fly, or get emotional when it's inappropriate.

I used to pray a lot to get help understanding emotions. I didn't want my wounded Emotional Body running my life because when I did that, it wasn't pleasant. All the words coming through my group tapping kept saying that God didn't make a mistake on emotions, and sure enough, my prayers were answered when I found Karla McLaren's book, *The Language of Emotions; What Your Feelings Are Trying to Tell You.* From her teaching, when I am talking to someone who's angry, I now know how to respond to their emotions without getting emotionally reactive. When I see anger, I can hold a vibe of compassion through alignment to my personal mission statement. I internally name, validate, and bless the emotional energy and its message, so the person in anger can choose whether to shift that energy. And even if they don't, I don't suffer from emotional pain since I don't entrain to the resonance of anger. I can respond with words that are appropriate to an angry person because I understand the message of the energy that's motivating the anger they feel. Even if they don't entrain to my consciousness, the process is transformative for me because of all the anger I have witnessed and experienced in the past. Now, I get to show up in my new resonance of not reacting to anger and instead respond proactively in consciousness. It's the transformation of reactive energy to proactive energy.

You can respond appropriately to another person's emotions when you understand the message in that emotion. Emotions are real. If someone is in anger, you don't want to shush them or tell them that they will get over it because that hurts your relationships and makes your communication less effective. Instead, you can validate them to rebuild trust and make amends if you wronged someone.

If someone is sad, you can have compassion and show up with love in every interaction you have. Sadness is about letting go of something. Listen with your heart without rushing or trying to fix the situation with words and help them let go when they are ready to ask for help.

When in a conflict, it can be hard to understand how to move the conversation forward, and one way to do that is to compassionately consider what's a win-win. You can also keep the end in mind and consider the impact of the emotions in the moment, balanced with what both parties deserve from the encounter. If I am in grief, that's not a good time to make decisions. I may not want to speak in a moment of anger because I can cause more harm. What experience do I deserve? I don't want to traumatize myself or anyone else. Get help and support to get what you want and evolve yourself.

Your healthy Emotional Body is always going to serve you well with its messages to strategically make intelligent decisions for what you want to consciously create. If your Emotional Body is wounded, you simply and painfully create more drama and trauma. Ever wonder how you or people you know keep attracting partners with the same issues? If you have an unresolved emotional pattern, you will attract people to your life to recreate that emotional pattern until you change your energy field.

Often, students will describe what they don't like about someone that bothers them, and when I write a list of the adjectives they state, suddenly, they see the bigger picture. What I write might look to them like a description of one of their parents, and they can see the old pattern they are re-experiencing. If you're in resistance, you won't be able to transform what you want to change, and the four steps for conscious creation won't be as successful as you'd like. When fear arises, and you choose courage instead of giving in to the fear, you begin to transform that energy. Do it often enough and you evolve the energy from fear into courage and then confidence.

Consciously Create Your Win-Wins—*Helen*

As mentioned in the first chapter, you consciously create a win-win to WIN. When you bless your life and others, you create a ripple of positivity across the planet. Your ripple effect of win-wins can extend through your circle of influence and even beyond. So, to create this positive vibration, consider how your actions and decisions affect everyone else involved. This applies to negotiations and deals in business, as well as parenting, friendships, and simple interactions with strangers. Those interactions happen every day and give us the opportunity to either decide to be selfish (and then entitlement or regret creep in), to be selfless (and then martyrdom sets in), or to find that perfect win-win.

Let's take Covey's win-win concept from *7 Habits* and apply it to Vibrational Law. Vibrationally, it's important to have clarity that what you're doing is in congruence with what you want and why. In other words, does one action or another better fit your mission and purpose? Ask yourself:

- *How do I benefit?* AND
- *How does it benefit and bless others?*

When you come to a situation with love, you're more likely to consciously create results that benefit you and others more in a win-win, as opposed to when you come with fear, which tends to separate us from others and limit blessings in a win-lose.

Here's a win-win that's happening in our mass consciousness and makes me really excited. There's so much free information available on the internet. The free flow of information is possible because of a new, evolving mindset that there's more than enough for everyone. Experts now freely share many of their best ideas. YouTube offers free teaching from experts and even people who are just a little further along the learning curve on everything—music, home repair, art, self-growth, etc. When we share what we know, we create win-win-wins.

This win/win concept can be especially tough for entrepreneurs and healers. I had trouble accepting money when I first started energy healing, because I felt like I was taking it from them, and then the clients wouldn't have enough money. That kind of thinking misses the whole boat. You can never be sick enough to make someone else well, and you can never be poor enough to make someone else financially secure. When you accept a fair price for services or goods, you are giving in return for the payment, and that's an exchange of energy that's balanced for a win-win in giving and receiving.

It was a big journey for me to come out of that mentality of scarcity of resources, and using my thoughts to change my perspective was the key. I had to learn to see the abundance around me. With practice, it became a very big vibrational shift for me. Now, being around others in success is very joyous to me. It's the opposite of the "you have-I don't have" outlook.

Win-lose can also occur when you feel resentful, cheated, or angry while you're employing conscious creation. It can happen on either side of a deal if you think someone didn't pay you enough, or if you believe you did more than they did. Feeling like a loser can also affect your physical health in ways related to stress, sleep, chronic pain, and more. You're responsible for how you feel, so it's logical to use the mind as a tool to feel good about your experience of you. Take a second and let that sink in. You can think differently and evolve your mind out of win-lose consciousness.

Sometimes when you struggle to find your win-win in a situation, you might look to see whether you're coming from a limited consciousness. Having a limited consciousness doesn't mean you're lazy or slow. Instead, it's about missing a piece of information. In any given moment, you're one field of complex layers of frequencies, and a limited consciousness might mean you need to tap into another layer. If you want something you don't have, you have to find new information in order to expand your mind, which will give you space for the new consciousness to have what you want.

The win-lose mentality is about scarcity-consciousness. If you see people with nice cars, homes, and vacations and feel bad, that's because you think if they have those things, you will never be able to have them for yourself. This mentality stems from a lack of self-worth, knowledge, and opportunity. A person in a win-lose mentality sees the world as a zero-sum game. It's an underlying belief system that there is not enough. You can also choose to see people having nice things and be happy for them, while feeling grateful for all the nice things you have in your life. For me, this took purposeful effort to practice at first.

Then, a decade later, my son noticed how my husband and I have a win-win attitude with paying his college tuition, and his sharp observation delightfully blew my mind. He noticed that many of the wealthy parents of his classmates were resentful of college costs and would make jokes and complaints, and yet we don't. Those parents were operating within a win-lose consciousness, despite having wealth. Believe me, I don't like the cost of tuition or taxes, etc., and yet my dominant resonance is, "Yay, we can give this gift of a college education to our child." I know that paying his tuition also blesses the college staff and others, including future students and all those lives their future jobs bless, too.

We feel that it's a win-win-win, not that the college is taking our money and we are losing somehow. It's also a win that we have the money to give him a good college education. My husband and I started managing our money late in life, and yet we accomplished this goal through our adherence to Vibrational Law, particularly standing in gratitude and using our minds as tools to live within our budget and make investments. My son felt only the dominant energy of win-win-win surrounding the cost of college. While he had to stick to a monthly budget, he knew we felt that we were giving him a gift. And he recently graduated from college without any debt. That is Vibrational Law in action.

An example of win-win-win I really enjoy is presented in *The Voice*. If you haven't seen it, this is a reality show with accomplished singers that mentor would-be singers. Although there is an elimination and competition element in the program, that isn't the point. The show supports and encourages young artists to develop their talents. With *The Voice*, all the contestants are winners, because they're learning and trying, and the show consistently frames itself in that way.

Post Notes—*Helen*

Everything on Earth was created the same way: with clarity of thought, belief, action, and consistency. We wouldn't have airplanes if the Wright brothers hadn't pushed through two failed attempts and a host of setbacks that they could've seen as reasons not to proceed. Even more impressive, Thomas Edison had 1,000 failed experiments before he actually got a light bulb to light up.

In both instances, the inventors knew what they wanted to create, believed in themselves and their tools of knowledge and access to materials. They were constantly doing everything they could, continued to do so until they had their breakthroughs, and then continued long after as they refined and mass-produced their inventions.

The four questions below are the short version of utilizing all seven principles when you are skilled in using them. The clarity it creates means you are utilizing LOA logically and consistently.

1. *What*: This asks for your **end in mind**. When you live the principles, your **end in mind** naturally includes **win/win/win** and is in your business, which creates **Clarity of Thought.**

2. *Why*: This question helps you be sure you're in your business. With the gifts of **synergy** and **win/win/win** it is beneficial to remain in your business which creates **Clarity of Belief.**

3. *How*: This asks for the action items, measurable goals and timelines for all of the steps necessary for success. It naturally includes **first things first, sharpen the saw**, being **proactive, win/win/win, seek to understand,** and possibly how you would be understood. **This question creates Clarity of Action and Consistency.**

4. *How will you know you're successful*: This question asks for your benchmarks against which you will test your "How" action items, above. It provides the ultimate alignment with clarity that makes you a vibrational match to consistent good, which shows up through synchronistic occurrences and events to support your goal.

CHAPTER 12

CLARITY AND CONSISTENCY CREATE YOUR BEST OUTCOME

Why Don't I Have My Best Outcome Right Now?—Cindy

As I worked with Helen, I became excited about consciously creating, but I noticed that things were still not going exactly as I wanted them to. I was trying to use her formula to finish her book and continue attracting clients, and my success was a mixed bag. I was making enough money, yet the book wasn't going as quickly as I wanted it to, and after my assistant quit, I was overwhelmed. I wondered why I created that for myself, so I asked Helen.

"One big reason that might happen is that you still harbor some resistance to what you're trying to consciously create at some level. You might also be going into judgment or trying to control the 'how' or 'when' you get that desired result," she said. Bingo! I wanted it all now. I didn't have a single goal that wasn't tied to the when AND the how.

I hadn't anticipated that the material would be so challenging for me to understand. After all, I have written for two neuroscientists and found that only moderately difficult. Helen's book was something different altogether. I would frequently be working on her book and be so overwhelmed by an idea or concept that I would almost pass out at my computer and have to lie down on the chaise lounge in my home office.

That was happening because my mind would need to take a break and absorb the information in my sleep where I could process it without my conscious mind getting in my own way. And sometimes when I had a breakthrough, it would be a few days before I had the courage to return to the manuscript and almost certainly experience the same thing again. But I knew it was worth it because I was starting to see how my life was changing for the better when I used her advice, and I wanted to help her bring this message to a bigger audience to help more people.

"I thought it was smart to have SMART goals that are specific, measurable, achievable, realistic, and trackable. How does that add up?" I asked.

"It's good to be specific, yet don't be tied to an arbitrary goal you set for yourself, like a deadline that's not about something real like tax season, etc. Also, try being open to different ways that you might also get what you want, besides the 'how' in your SMART goals," she said. "Also, it sounds like you might be confusing goal-setting with manifesting. Manifesting is about creating something new that's outside the expected norm. We might save that for another book, too."

"Okay, I'll keep that in mind now. I think I should change my goal for completing your book. Instead of, 'I will write Helen's bestseller in 6 months,' maybe I should say, 'I will write Helen's bestseller in the least amount of time and to its best possible version to accomplish her mission.'"

"Or, is it 'our mission?' Let's go through some of those possible scenarios and then create a winning plan to be the best version of you."

Remove the Filter of Resistance—*Helen*

Resistance is the projection of no-energy (rejection) that says something has to change and can't be the way it is. That no-energy depletes your power by keeping you in the problem instead of stepping out into the solution. Resistance persists when there's a filter (which is a belief system) running in your background that doesn't match where you want to go next. And the solution can be as simple as staying in your business or choosing love. Or the solution can be bigger, like choosing what you want and deciding how to get it. Regardless, resistance means being stuck; it is the opposite of solution energy. Until you can accept things as they are, you cannot create a solution.

You can get out of resistance by creating a bigger story or paradigm. For me, that's seeing through a much larger perspective than my own, one that tells me that there is a Divine Intelligence, that I don't understand how it works completely, that I don't have to agree with everything, and that I can take my focus to my circle of influence and not worry about all the things I can't control. Sometimes it's really fast, and sometimes I have to diligently work to align.

For example, my mom was resisting aging. She complained all the time: Her body didn't work well, she didn't want to use a walker, and she didn't want help for all these things she needed help with. Her eyesight deteriorated to the point that she couldn't read, and with her Parkinson's, she couldn't write either. Then two years later, my dad was bedridden; my mom didn't have her car anymore, but she'd adapted to her new reality. She was taking care of my dad. She'd let go of her resistance to the degree that she didn't even remember her old complaints. And guess what? Now she can read and write again and gets around with her walker.

You can't fix a problem if you don't accept that the problem exists. It's not that you're accepting a bad outcome by accepting the problem;

you're accepting the reality of the situation. From there, you will become empowered to seek out and implement solutions.

For everything that's a part of you, all your bodies have to match up, as we will discuss in Chapter 15. So, if something is out of alignment, that energy has to bubble up to the surface to be transformed and evolved before you can keep moving forward. If you don't address it, and instead shove whatever it is back beneath the surface, it won't go away. You inadvertently give it more power to bubble up again and again.

Harness Preference Over Judgement—*Helen*

We talked about judgment earlier and how it can be triggered, and let's look a little closer about how it affects your conscious creation. Judgment is a restrictive energy that limits and separates you because it is fear-based. Instead, it's helpful to use preference to choose what you want and then discernment to avoid imposing your preferences on others.

If you go to a lunch buffet, you don't want to spend the whole time looking at everything you don't want; rather, you look for the foods you want to eat and enjoy them. The judgment of going through and pointing out everything you don't want limits, distracts, and changes your brain chemistry. In the same way, if you're dealing with a difficult parent who is trying to connect and yet, maybe has terrible follow-through, you have a choice. You can either give into judgment and stand in your hurt feelings, or you can exercise discernment and focus on her attempt to connect to you, thereby receiving the love and attention that is there, simply by receiving what is given.

When "should" enters your vocabulary, that's a good cue you're not in preference. If you write a book, and put your heart into it, you will still probably get a bad review or two. Judgment would say, "What's wrong with these people?" In contrast, Discernment says, "Wow, I did such a good job with my message that all but a few people found something helpful in this book." Feel the difference?

When you don't get what you want, it's not because you're bad, stupid, lazy, or slow. Instead, you're missing some pieces of information that would help you expand your consciousness. Your belief system fits the consciousness you're in, and to expand your beliefs, you have to up-level your consciousness. Your weaknesses from the past, or the present, can be turned into your greatest strengths. Great leaders often come from being victimized and then go into a powerful, creative energy. They have the capacity to go from that victim consciousness into a powerful leader consciousness for the whole planet.

Work the Tricky, Fine Edge Between Surrendering and Intending—*Helen*

When I talk about surrendering and intending, this is another way of saying, "no attachment to the outcome." You want to create desire through imagination, affirmation, and right action. Feed that desire and hold positive expectation, and don't be attached to the outcome. Enjoy the feeling when you imagine that you already have what you want.

Your power is in the present moment, as you might have heard before. Then, how do you visualize the future while being fully present? If you write and read your vivid vision, stay in the prayer of faith, and get your 7 Bodies aligned with having what you want, then you're surrendering to the process in the present moment. When you get really good at this, you can create the feeling place of having what you want, without yet having the outcome.

When you do affirmations and vision boards, have in your mind, 'this or something better,' to soften your attachment. In healing work and prayer, people who pray for a higher intelligence's will to be done have better results than people who pray for a specific outcome. You can see work from Dr. Joe Dispenza and Gregg Braden to find out more.

In terms of remaining unattached to a specific result, timing is another facet of conscious creation that differs from setting goals. With goal setting, you would generally want to set an achievable end-date to hold yourself accountable. An example is expecting your weight loss to reach 0.5-2 lbs. per week so that, in 2-3 months, you can lose 10 lbs. when you consistently follow a plan. In contrast, with conscious creation, it's not helpful to be tied to the when or how. You want to consistently follow principle-based thinking and then continue creating that new pattern for as long as it takes to bring your idea into existence. Thus, instead of weight loss, a goal of healing your body to get off diabetes medication is one that you wouldn't want to put a time limit on.

When I teach, I stay in my business. I have no control over whether the student understands, follows through or continues with classes. I can only manage how I show up and my intention, presence, commitment, and level of integrity. I surrender to that and let go of micromanaging how others receive. This makes me much more empowered in my giving.

It's tricky if you don't believe in something bigger than you. Control is fear-based, and surrender is faith-based. Rarely does this show up as powerfully as it does regarding health, because we really want ourselves and those we love to pull through. If a client asks me, before surgery, to do a clearing for them, I do so for the staff, technology, and the room. I call in angels to support them and the nurses and surgeons. If they desire, I also give them a thorough tapping session or hypnosis recording for receiving all the good energy of a surgery in alignment to healing. Those actions are intending, and then you surrender to whatever happens. Afterwards, whatever happens, choose how to show up in that reality.

Surrendering doesn't mean doing nothing. You simply give up the attachment to the 'how' and 'when' the goal is achieved, even as you take consistent right action to bring your intention to fruition. This is tricky because it's different from goal-setting. When creating (drawing to ourselves) something that doesn't yet exist, we don't have control over how or when it arrives.

I Fully Intend to Surrender—Oops!—*Cindy*

Surrender has always been a tough concept for me. I thought about how this compared to my process of, "bless and release." I don't remember the first place I read about this, but the gist is this: You bless something that's not working for you, whether it's a relationship, job, etc., and then release it by detaching from the outcome. I would use bless and release when someone let me down and I decided to end the relationship and cut cords.

I asked Helen if she thought what I was doing was enough of a surrender.

"When you release them," she asked, "do they always go?"

"Sometimes at first, but then for some of those people, they come back later. If they've worked on what bugged me, I gladly give them another chance, except for one lady who broke up another friend's marriage. That really upsets me, and I would rather not see her and be reminded of how much pain that caused everyone. I have run into her twice in two different countries. It's quite bizarre."

"What happened when you saw her?" Helen pressed.

Each time I saw her, my hands went clammy, and I felt my heart race. I wanted to hide from her, but I didn't. I thought she should hide from me, but she didn't. She said, "Hi," to me, and I would hug her. I didn't feel the hug. I would be gracious and polite, like a good southern lady, and end the interaction as quickly as possible, with no promise of follow up.

Helen suggested that maybe that friend needs something from me that I'm not giving her, and that's why she keeps popping up. Maybe it's not enough for me to be polite and act "nice." Maybe I need to dig deep and find a way to truly be compassionate. I am not there yet, although I definitely get the idea. I have so much personal growth left to do!

Be the Best Version of You with Conscious Presence—*Helen*

Mindfulness can be brought to anything you're doing, like washing dishes or taking a walk, and that's not exactly what I mean by "conscious presence." Conscious presence is about anchoring into presence and choosing to be mindful and stay in your body, choosing to observe yourself and be in the experience—in other words, observing your own mindfulness.

When you're working consciously with the observer, that's the soul self. You can pause and be thoughtful before reacting and think of what result you want, so you take action that syncs up in that direction. This is a powerful skill to have in our age of digital communication, when a hurt feeling can quickly turn into an angry email or text that you can't take back after others read it.

We tend to think of higher and lower, like levels in a high rise building and up-leveling, and yet, the E's talk about expansion out into all directions. I'm not going up and leaving anything below me. Rather, I am expanding to encompass what I have and more. It's about wholeness. Conscious creation is about expanding your consciousness to include the new things, as opposed to attracting things. When you transform sadness into closure, or evolve disappointment into new levels of appreciation, you aren't letting go, you're gaining life experience, growth, accomplishment, acceptance, ease or completion. The transformation creates more space for more of what you want.

In my community, I see energy healers trying to get rid of the bad, and what you really want to do is transform energy and evolve your patterns to create a new dominant resonance. I transformed my past so much that I keep the knowledge and experience from it, and it prompts me to want things in a different way, as Joseph Campbell describes in *The Hero's Journey*. At the same time, I didn't get rid of my past, because as people, we need the richness of our struggles to grow.

CHAPTER 13

CHOOSE LOVE INSTEAD OF FEAR

The Best and Hardest Game—Helen

When negative emotions surface, they present an opportunity to go deep into ourselves and take an honest look at what's really going on. Then we can choose to transform the beliefs beneath the emotions into beliefs that could give us what we prefer. For most of my students, this is hard and uncomfortable work, so I urge you to remember what's on the other side of the effort you're putting forth. What is your life going to be like when problem X is evolved, and you can think about it and feel nothing except gratitude? That is a powerful freedom that you can consciously create when you transform fear-based emotions into love.

Love is the best game and hardest one you can play on Earth.

Think About a Problem with Gratitude? I Don't Think So...—*Cindy*

We put Helen first in this chapter because for this topic, I didn't bring many preconceived ideas to the conversation. I didn't know enough about fear and love to have any ideas about how they related to each other at all. So, when Helen started answering my questions, I was caught off-guard.

After all, aren't I afraid sometimes for good reasons? I remembered when we moved to Malaysia and I was mugged within the first month. Before that happened, I hadn't been afraid, but afterward, I was terrified for a long time that it would happen again. And I found out that it was a common occurrence; most local women I met had been mugged 2-3 times. I felt powerless and justified to be afraid that it might happen again.

Why should I be grateful that I was mugged? I had already recognized that I was in a low vibration at the moment when I had been mugged, and I had gotten over feeling like a victim by studying PTSD and how I had suffered from that afterward. I still hated the two men who came up behind me; one jumped off the scooter, the other drove ahead of me, then the guy who got off the bike sprinted toward me and grabbed my pink Marc Jacobs handbag that had the only key to my apartment, car, and all my 2 credit cards in it (no money, by the way). I screamed, pulled it back, and held on for dear life as he dragged me a few feet down the dirty broken sidewalk.

That was the only time I was mugged there. In time, I learned how the local women took precautions to be less of a target, like not wearing a necklace (muggers will snap it off your neck), carrying my bag on the inside arm facing away from the street if I was going to carry one, not carrying a handbag and putting my phone and wallet in a plastic shopping bag if I was going to walk on a sidewalk, and looking out for suspicious activity.

So, how did that experience fit into Helen's concept of love and fear? It took me quite a way into the editing process to figure it out.

Love Vs. Fear—*Helen*

Love and fear are the biggest creative forces on Earth that we know of. Love connects, and fear separates. Love is expansive and open, and fear contracts, attacks or withdraws. Fear can cause one to freeze, faint, flee, or fight. Freeze is going unconscious and being unable to respond. Fainting is representative of us mentally separating from our bodies. Fleeing is running away, self-sabotage, breaking up, or ceasing communication. Fighting is attacking, arguing, or resisting change. Fear is feeling victimized and disempowered. Love is trusting and expansive—feeling safe and sharing with respect and thoughtfulness.

As you can see, love and fear are also the biggest opposites imaginable. From fear stem the other lower vibe emotions like anger. If you search beneath your anger, you will find a fear that either things will never be fair, boundaries will never be safe, or trust will never be restored. There's also grief, which is sometimes similar. It's a natural process that can lead to the fear you won't ever feel good again without a person and their love, or without a job and its fulfillment, etc. Fear is the feeling that you lost something you cannot have back. In other words, fear is the big separator between people, as well as between ourself and our inner peace.

Love is the big connector. For instance, let's think about parenting. If you parent from a place of fear, your Mommy-Ego, which is the fear that others will judge you for your child's behavior, is the driver. Let's say you're shopping, and your child is throwing a tantrum because you won't buy him a toy. Your Mommy-Ego will cause you to react to your child's age-appropriate behavior with hitting, yelling, or berating. In contrast, parenting from a place of love will cause you to react by understanding age-appropriate behavior and responding to it that way, by acknowledging the child's feelings, explaining so he understands, and kindly and creatively diverting his attention.

Fear creates war, disease, sickness, and fights. As an emotion, it is telling you to pay attention because you don't have enough information. If you feel fear regularly, it's a pattern, perhaps because you feel disconnected and unsupported. In contrast, love is the strongest energy on Earth, and it's the only thing that's kept us from killing ourselves as a species. With love as a dominant pattern, your joy is not contingent on outside forces, and it's all within your power to create and share as much as you want from an eternal power supply.

It can be tough to put love over fear into practice though. Once, a student said that at work she was told she shouldn't wear her heart on her sleeve. She was trying to figure out how to stop being triggered into fear-mode when co-workers criticized her work, and I helped her see that the way to endure criticism is not to be cut off from your emotions and instead to learn about and through them. Your heart is patience, courage, curiosity, and forgiveness, which are what we wish everyone would be. What you don't want to wear on your sleeve is your wounded Emotional Body.

In conversations about love, I often get questions about unconditional love. On this plane of existence, unconditional love doesn't exist for most people, so they misinterpret it. On Earth, we love better with boundaries. When you love without using the mind as a tool, you might mean well, and then it ends horribly. When you love with the mind as a tool, you are being strategic and logical, and it doesn't allow the heart to be manipulated. For instance, I love my children, although their definition might be: *If I love them, I wouldn't send them to school.* So, love expressed as a parent is: *I make sure you're a high-functioning human.*

If you only pour love out to someone, that's probably co-dependency, because they can't receive it very well. If you use the mind without the heart, that usually ends in a misuse of power, like manipulation, or staying in the tangible instead of intangible. For the first time in human history, many of us aren't worrying about food or safety, so we can evolve our hearts. When you use the mind as a tool and understand principle-based thinking, you can access heart-energy and have a wonderful experience being in human form.

We're here to play with love in this dimension and have a great experience. I didn't understand this until I saw with my own kids that the payoff is great, and then I wanted more of it. Love connects you to more good. Fear separates you from more good. In the stock market, the larger the risk, the larger the potential payoff. If you're too fearful and can't be strategic about losses, you will play small and not have your biggest possibility. If you're creative and are fearful about what others will think, you'll never reach your potential as an artist. Fear limits, and love connects you to more good.

The next time you're in fear-mode, get curious and try to find out what you don't know. If you feel fear, find out what's smart. Is it appropriate to develop courage? If you want to cross the freeway and feel fear, that's beneficial fear. Then, you want to choose intelligence and courage. Courage would be asking directions on how to get to the other side or asking for help. If you're afraid for your job at work because they installed an HR executive as Vice President of your division, bless them and get a meeting with them. In the meeting, ask questions about what their plans are, and take appropriate action to stay or go on your own terms, knowing that everything that's happening is to bless you.

I Think I Did Create a New Pattern, Eventually—*Cindy*

So, I said that I was only mugged the one time. Why didn't that become a repeating pattern? Like I said earlier, I started doing things differently. I learned and applied new safety tips for Malaysia that don't apply to safety in America. Another thing that changed is that for about a year after the incident, I couldn't stop talking about it. I was so angry and scared. Helen talks about trust and how fear is partly about not trusting that the bad thing won't happen or won't happen again. I didn't trust that the safety precautions I was taking were enough, and I took a self-defense class and got a hand-held weapon for my keyring.

Finally, after telling my story over and over and hearing so many other women's stories, I started to tell my story differently, in a way that helped the listener instead of whining "why me?!" Another thing that changed is that I decided to quit being miserable at home all the time and volunteered to be the Membership Director for the American Association of America. I started helping newly arrived expat women to start out knowing what I didn't, and it was my job to help them meet other people and discover Kuala Lumpur, hopefully to have a great experience. And, I started having a better experience too. Three and half years into our posting, I truly loved Malaysia, its people, and even its problems, because I didn't feel victimized anymore.

I learned that the crime rings are mostly Indonesian syndicates, so I dropped my anger toward Malaysians, but I also learned how poor and desperate the Indonesian immigrants were. That doesn't make the theft okay (plus, they didn't really get anything valuable unless they were going to resell the used handbag, and they usually even toss the Louis Vuitton's). The violence of dragging me down the sidewalk is definitely not okay, yet I saw where that fit into the larger culture. And, all the good things about Malaysia—like the amazing good food, opportunities to help local charities, participating in the Malaysian running group and meeting real friends there— overshadowed the one bad incident that I was empowered to avoid.

"Do you see that you stopped showing up in fear and started showing up in love?" Helen asked.

"I think so. I stopped telling the story from a place of fear and started telling it from a place of care for the listener. And, after a while, I had so many better stories of good things that I hardly ever wanted to tell that story unless safety came up and I thought it would help someone for me to share it."

Now, Let's Focus on Love—*Helen*

When you understand how vibration works, and choose higher vibrations of love, it's so miraculous and astounding. By emitting the frequency of love, true vibration and connection, your field will bring more of what you want into it. When you live in a pattern of fear, then everything the universe wants to bless you with is limited. All emotion seeks to motivate you to a certain response.

Fear motivates you to get more information, and love motivates you to connect to good. As a mother, I want my children to have good self-esteem. So, I never belittle them, say "no" without a reason, and I don't make my displeasure about them, I make it clear I'm unhappy regarding their actions or lack of action. That's the alignment of self-esteem to action and words, and it gets you to the target of true love better than yelling or smacking, which might get the immediate change wanted, yet doesn't produce love.

When you choose love instead of fear, you must work on surrendering to something bigger, like God or fate, after you set your intention for the highest good. If your loved one has a disease, you would use your mind to discern what's in your control and what isn't. How do you align to faith and love instead of fear? You're prompted to be an emotional being, so when fear comes up, recognize that fear and then choose faith, and be grateful for all the tools you can practice consistently. And then, choose love. Love of self, others and life as it is. Even if you don't get this job, that invitation to speak, or the title of winner, your disappointment will be lighter when you surrender to the reality that life is bigger than any one of us and our personality's immediate desires. There is a Divine Plan, and it is complex and organized.

Post Note—*Helen*

Speaking the language of the Divine by being the resonance of love is the **end in mind**. This aim requires you to **seek to understand** what love is, and isn't, *to others* so you can be in balance with giving and receiving love.

Now that I know love is the transformer of lower vibes, I am committed to developing mastery with choosing "love" over "fear." Before I understood this vibrationally, I never witnessed or experienced the payoff of doing so in real time to create **win/win/wins**.

I do so by **sharpening the saw** via continuing to read books on love and transforming fear, which is also **proactive** and keeping the **end in mind**. This constant learning allows me to choose thoughts, words, and actions that align vibrationally to love. The **synergy** created from those efforts is always **win/win/win**. **First things first** usually involves being **proactive** enough to stop reactions, even as I feel the fear, and remain in choice of how I show up. Check out Cindy's foreword for her beautiful example of this.

CHAPTER 14

ENERGETIC LEGACY

The Long Line of Inherited Crap—Cindy

When we sat down to talk about energetic legacies, I was armed with so many wounds, I think they were practically actually oozing. I thought "energetic legacies" meant the pattern of abuse that's often passed down from one generation to the next.

I have a personal grudge against this entire phenomenon, because I was born into a legacy of physical and emotional abuse that pushed me to almost kill myself when I was only 12 years old. Still, I was stoked to understand it better, because my goal is to stop those cycles in my bloodline. "Okay, Helen. When you help people work on their 'energetic legacies,' what's that about for you?"

"It's about that quotation, 'Be the change you want to see in the world,' by Gandhi." I like that quote too, so I nodded.

"All our movies and stories are about this pattern, as explained in Joseph Campbell's *The Hero's Journey*," Helen continued. "You're either the hero or victim of your own life. This can be awful when the buck stops with you, or it can be empowering."

It certainly could be awful. I finally got a sort of handle on this idea when I was in therapy and came to the concept that I can't change the past, or certainly not other peoples' behavior, although I could choose what I did about it. "Okay, but what about when children are harmed? When adults behave badly to other adults, I agree that you

133

have agency, yet as a kid, your options are limited, as is your brain development."

"I can, and will, address that concern, and I have done so before, for my own life, and my students with early family trauma. First, let's get some foundational ideas in place, so my explanation makes more sense," Helen said.

"Sounds good," I said. I was so ready to get a handle on this once and for all.

"Like Vibrational Law, you're creating your energetic legacy whether you're aware of it or not. When I bless myself by having the best experience of me, I bless every life I interact with. That's an energetic legacy."

That was interesting. I hadn't known that energetic legacies were anything other than family line issues. I paused and thought about what my own energetic legacy might be. "I try to always send good energy when I interact with people, even looking into the eyes of a cashier at H.E.B. and making her feel like I mean I want her to have a good day." Finally, maybe here was a LLOA component I was doing right.

"When you do your own personal spiritual growth, you're helping to change mass-consciousness. You're either adding to or subtracting from victim consciousness. Every time you ask for forgiveness or forgive, you're affecting the whole soup of mass-consciousness."

Oh, man. There was that f-word again. It was time to buckle my seatbelt, start asking questions, and type.

Energetic Legacy—*Helen*

The energetic legacy of my family living through the war was awful, and they had fears that carried on long after the events they lived through. My mother had fertility problems, and so did I. A person can inherit physical traits, energetic patterns and unresolved emotions. Because I personally chose to change my energy, my kids will have different energy around money and health. My parents didn't have the choices to study the things I have studied. It's not that any of us are right or wrong, it's more about deciding what's your preference and developing your skill for conscious co-creation.

"The mind is a great servant, but not a great master." Robin Sharma

We are here in form experiencing ourselves as separate from others, yet truly we are all part of the whole of creation. There is never a time that we are not giving and receiving from the whole at one, or many, vibrational levels. I often ask myself, is what I am resonating through my thoughts, words and actions what I feel good about as my contribution to all that is?

Through epigenetics[15], we see that the pattern repeats itself until someone transforms it with consciousness. We all come in with this energy from our ancestors, like a genetic legacy for skin and hair color. The phrase, "the sins of the father," does apply, although then children are all different, so everyone in the family doesn't have exactly equal parts of each bit of inheritance. Patterns repeat all the time. Until you show up in an old consciousness and choose to act, speak, and think differently (apply a new consciousness), the pattern keeps repeating. This relates to inherited patterns about money, creativity, health, relationships, etc.

---

[15] Epigenetics: A means in which trapped emotions can be passed on from one generation to the next.

Your energetic legacy also impacts how you contribute to Mass Consciousness. If you are in patterns of addiction, fear, judgment, etc., then that's what you're contributing to mass consciousness. What are you paying forward? Covey talks about writing your mission statement and your eulogy—are you energetically aligned to them?

I worked with a gentleman in a private session who said he was doing everything right and yet couldn't get to the next level of promotion in his job. He was taking right action and thinking correctly. I asked him how old he was and how his father's life had been at that age. It turned out that at that age, the economy had changed, and his father had lost his business and income—at that time, the client was 15. Upon reaching the age at which his dad had lost his business, the client was feeling limitation and stagnation. EFT cleared that inherited energy, and then he continued to up-level professionally.

Another gentleman found me online looking for EFT. We looked at his father's story and discovered that his father had died three years before his own age. He realized that he had started waiting to die and reliving the energetic pattern of not living any more or enjoying the things he used to enjoy. This reminded me of Mark Wolynn's *It Didn't Start with You*. Wolynn shares that sometimes people are stuck in a grief pattern and can't figure out what they're grieving, and they figure out that in gestation their mother was grieving, and they had taken that on, too. It's easy to forget to look at unresolved energetic patterns when something elusive happens and we're not getting what we want or want to feel out of it.

Without repeating patterns, we couldn't exist in the reality we're all co-creating with our perceptions and filters. Our world wouldn't be stable without repeating patterns. With LOA, if you created everything you think of, what a mismatch that would be when you consider all the random thoughts you think in any one day. So, only the consistent pattern will take form. How long and how many people share the pattern relates to how quickly the pattern can be transformed.

Is This How My Friend is Literally a Pain in My Neck?—*Cindy*

So, I mentioned before that I had a lot of neck pain while we were working on this book. I've had neck pain in the past, but at one point during the writing of this book, it was so bad that I couldn't lift my arms or get out of bed.

I was in the process of being in an old pattern with a person from my past, and trying to show up differently. The work I was doing was mostly taking different action. So, when she did the things she always did, I was not doing the thing I had always done in response. I was making different choices to change the pattern, and my neck pain was at its worst. In our video conferences, Helen would see me constantly rubbing my neck and moving my head to try to get some relief.

"So, for the energetic legacy, I think this person is literally being a pain in my neck. I'm not doing what she wants me to do in our co-dependent relationship, so she sent me neck pain." I expected Helen to agree, and instead, she laughed. It wasn't a mean laugh, more like a surprised one.

"Your friend can't send you energy unless you're open to it," she said.

"It is real, though, right? I have read about this before where a pain in your body can be tied to an emotional event and not an actual injury or particular disease, or maybe there is a real problem, but traditional medicine doesn't help because it's an energy problem, too. Does that concept fit in here?"

"Oh, yes it does, Big Time," Helen said. I felt a little better. "Do you want to know what that pain in your neck really is?" I nodded.

"It's the emotion you feel toward her. I don't know if it's resentment, judgment, or what, and–"

"It's all that and more."

"Would you like to be in a place energetically where the next time she does the same thing, if she does, you'll feel nothing and won't even care?"

I definitely did, but that's what I thought I was doing with trying to show up in the old energy and acting differently, so I brought that up.

"The fact that you identified the pattern and are choosing different action is a great step," Helen continued. "If you want an even better experience of yourself in this pattern, you can also change your emotions. That way, when this happens, all those low vibrations aren't even triggered."

I tried to imagine what it would be like if she used her trigger words with me and I just wasn't triggered. It sounded good, but it also sounded hard to do. "What's the secret?"

"It's no secret. It's in most sacred and motivational teachings, although most people don't really understand it fully. You can practice forgiveness."

I should've seen that coming. My neck really hurt, and I wondered what would happen if I saw that pain as my own feelings, instead of feelings she made me feel. It was a powerful idea I would have to mull over.

Choice is Freedom—*Helen*

The Law of Attraction is often misunderstood in the context of energetic legacies going further forward or backward. If you had a difficult childhood, it can be very painful if someone says, "you chose your parents" or "you choose your struggles." What you attracted, in your ancestral legacy, is also about genetic coding, and repressed and unhealed emotions. So, the real question isn't, "why did you choose addiction." Instead, it's "which one of my selves picked this, and how can it serve me?" Selves might include personality, eternal soul self, child self, adult self, wounded self, creative self, etc., and we'll talk more about this in Chapter 15.

I love this quote from the film, *The Adjustment Bureau*. Matt Damon's character says, "Freewill is a gift you only get to use if you're willing to work for it." So, when you think, "why did I do something so dumb" or "why does it always turn out like this" consider that something else might be going on. That probably wasn't a choice, although it was a repeating pattern, and it might be from your ancestors and their repeating patterns. In a different dimension, your soul-self chooses the circumstances and energies to explore in human-form. You don't choose these repeating patterns from human personality; no one would consciously choose obesity, violence, addiction, et al. What you can choose is to work to change the pattern.

Skill to direct your thoughts (into alignment with what you prefer) is possible only if you are willing to be dedicated to developing it.

In a nutshell, real freedom is freedom from fear; always. When you can make a choice, you have some power, and you're not a victim. When you're a victim, you have no power or agency. There is a big difference between a choice to feel less bad (like dessert for dinner) and a choice to feel really good (like bless your food before you eat it and chew every bite). Choosing forgiveness, instead of resentment, is a lot of work, and it puts you in the energy of freedom from victim consciousness. Forgiveness is a pattern of choice to build into your biology and energetic field.

"You cannot get through a single day without having an impact on the world around you. What you do makes a difference, and you have to decide what kind of difference you want to make." - Jane Goodall

Post Notes—*Helen*

Seeking to understand the complexity of what we are, in human form, helps us understand LOA in a logical way. I found it impossible to see the logic behind something that didn't make sense in real-time. Realizing that everything energetic is about patterns and finding with clients and myself repeating patterns through generations led me to understanding the much bigger paradigm of energetic legacy, or epigenetics, which certainly confirmed the logic of LOA for me.

If you want to look into this topic further, check out Mark Wolynn's book: *It Didn't Start with You: How Inherited Family Trauma Shapes Who We Are* and *How to End the Cycle*.

I leave you with this quotation :

"We are slowed down sound and light waves, a walking bundle of frequencies tuned into the cosmos. We are souls dressed up in biochemical garments and our bodies are the instruments through which our souls play their music." (— unknown source)

CHAPTER 15

DISCOVER YOUR 7 BODIES

Finally! The Bodies!—Cindy

You've probably seen a few references to "the bodies" throughout this book. If you're curious what Helen means about them, well, I was too. Until the interview, I had some notes I put together from when she had occasionally referenced one body or another, but I hadn't known what they meant, or what all seven of them were, before we talked about them in detail.

I was very excited to finally get the scoop.

"So, what are the 7 Bodies?" I asked. As she listed them, my head started spinning. Some of them were familiar to me, but others weren't, and at first, I got hung up on how you can be a body of bodies. For Helen, that "how" turned out to be a tool to get to the "what."

"The more information you have," she said, "the more easily you can integrate all your bodies and see how each part fits together. This is especially true for understanding how truly complex we are, so we can use that knowledge to create fuller alignment and be better conscious creators," she said.

I mulled over that for a couple of weeks as I edited my notes and re-watched the recording of our interview. It blew my mind that what we normally think of as "mind-body-soul" could be further compartmentalized to seven parts. Once I understood the 7 Bodies,

I wondered why I had ever lumped them all together before. The way I used to think started to make less sense as I would try to access and think about my new 7 Bodies.

The Bodies—*Helen*

Someone masters a skill when they've been in many complex situations with the same teaching and application. That's no different with understanding the bodies than anything else. It's that expansion of experience that creates your mastery of them. At first, it's overwhelming, although, if you stick with it, you keep learning and picking up new things.

For instance, taking up running is not only about putting one foot in front of the other for a certain time at a certain speed. It's about having the right shoes and the right gait, as well as knowing how to stretch, cultivating the right mindset, engaging with your community, preparing pre-run meals, etc. Running also requires practicing several times a week in the same conditions with the same tools. Think of all those pieces of the running puzzle as "bodies." They encompass the body of information, as well the human body of the runner, body of gear, etc., and together, they are a complete picture of running, the full body. They're all available within the context of running, and the more of them you tap into, the higher your mastery.

This same paradigm works achieving a higher vibration or getting something else you want. You have a Physical Body, and that's not your only body. Within your complex self, you have several bodies that exist within different overlapping and co-existing layers. Bringing them into alignment with your mission, purpose, and goal in any situation is the next piece to master LLOA.

Thinking about yourself within the context of all your bodies helps you make sense of contradicting thoughts or feelings, as well as premonitions or intuitions that feel like they came from nowhere. And using all of these bodies helps you progress. However, they have to be used together to be an energetic match for consistent results. When you understand what you want that you don't have and then engage with it purposefully using all seven of the bodies, you can create what you want much faster. We're going to go over each of these bodies so you can understand and work with them to make sure they're all aligned to the outcome you prefer.

The bodies are:

1. Mental
2. Physical
3. Emotional
4. The Energetic Body/Auric Field
5. Spiritual Body
6. Karmic Body
7. Egoic Body

The Mental Body

Let's start with one you're quite familiar with—the Mental Body. In popular psychology, the mind, or Mental Body, is often broken into the conscious, unconscious, and subconscious:

- The **conscious** mind directs your focus and distinguishes between real and imagined thoughts.
- The **subconscious** stores short and long-term memories for recall.
- The **unconscious** mind stores repressed and automatic memories, and while these memories can be accessed with effort, they usually run in the background undetected.

All three of these consciousnesses comprise your Mental Body, which, if developed properly, can become an invaluable tool for your progress. If neglected, the Mental Body can work against your aims. As Robin Sharma's saying goes, "The mind is a wonderful servant but a terrible master."

To raise your vibration, you must better understand your Mental Body, and fortunately, this gets easier with practice. By choosing how to think and aligning your principle-based thoughts with your mission, you create the greatest possible outcome for yourself in every situation.

Imagine this: When you want to have a better experience of yourself, what if you can train your conscious mind to believe it's already real—not imagined—then, you can build your subconscious mind with the information to support yourself in that reality when it presents itself, and you can keep your unconscious from running a counter-argument in the background. That's what I mean by aligning all of your Mental Body.

Physical Body

Your Physical Body is the physical manifestation of your dominant vibration. This includes your karmic energy, genetics, belief patterns because the Physical Body holds all this information. It also expresses your emotions physically, including any PTSD or unresolved emotional trauma. The Physical Body can also change dramatically. For example, as Deepak Chopra teaches in many of his talks, your liver is completely new every 90 days. Every 11 months, your skeletal system is completely new.

The Physical Body is not fully understood. There's no one diet, supplement, operation, or solution to heal everyone because we are so complex. When you are on a diet, it will only work when you believe it will work and feed your mind with success stories from people who believe in the diet. If you don't hold your own belief system firmly, and you allow your conviction to slip, you will find yourself plateauing. In turn, you will be susceptible to the mass consciousness assumption that gaining weight is inevitable. If you start dieting, plateau, and aren't engaged at all levels of being with what you want, you will fall off the wagon.

There's so much that we don't know about the Physical Body, and as our technology changes, so does our understanding of the human body. Back when they didn't understand germs, hospitals were very dangerous places; think about what's happened and what we've been able to accomplish by understanding germs. We're still learning about all these bodies, and it's best to use your mind to learn and make informed decisions.

Emotional Body

The Emotional Body is the big one on this plane of existence, in terms of being the stage through which God comes to explore. So, how do you explore your humanity and hold your spirituality? All emotions have information and intelligent messages to offer, so as they come up, good and bad, we can listen and learn from them and keep evolving.

On the surface, a lot of us would like to only experience positive emotions, although that's not how emotions work. I learned about emotions through the E's channeling words for EFT, which taught me that emotions are about contrasts: you can't choose love without having experienced fear, you wouldn't choose kindness if you didn't experience cruelty, etc. It's about evolving the skill of choice. Emotions aren't good or bad. They are all information and part of our humanity. Negative emotions invite me to do forgiveness work or to reach for a bigger perspective. I don't make the emotions wrong: once they serve me, they filter on through. It's only the emotions I've tried to avoid that dug in and created in my Physical Body.

Emotion is energy in motion. It's always a motivation for something. When you get the motivation from emotion, you want to be sure your mind is working as a tool to be proactive instead of reactive. You can be responsive from a bigger paradigm of what you want to experience versus reactive with the emotion.

Emotion is a universal language. We are emotionally driven creatures. All our movies and stories work because our experience of our emotions is similar. You're hardwired for emotion first, although we don't teach children anything beyond "use your head" and "don't spontaneously react 24/7," because kids have to be taught how to regulate emotions in order to function in society.

Interestingly enough, the Emotional Body is not separate from the Physical Body. To summarize Sigmund Freud, "Buried emotions are well-preserved." Emotional patterns can even repeat through many generations until consciousness is brought to them. The more ancestral energy that you can evolve the higher vibrations you create for your family after you.

So, how do you transform emotional energy? You have to show up in the old energy differently, whether it's yours or from your ancestors. You have to feel impatience in your Physical Body and mind to develop the skill of patience. After repeatedly showing up in the emotion of impatience and acting with patience, the latter becomes natural, and you adapt your Emotional Body and Physical Body to have the stamina of patience in times you would have previously felt and acted with impatience.

There are no bad emotions. Everything that happens can be an invitation and a gift for more good.

The Energetic Body/Auric Field

Have you ever felt someone stare at you? Their eyes aren't physically weighing you down, so what is it you're feeling? Have you ever been in a house where you immediately felt at ease, where you felt like you wanted to kick your shoes off and make yourself comfortable? What about a house where you felt stiff and cold, as if you shouldn't touch anything?

When you visit a hospital, the fluorescent lights are harsh, and it's unpleasant. In contrast, in the hospital's chapel, when you enter that space, it will feel still and peaceful. In all of these examples, those sixth sense feelings you get about other people or spaces are coming from your Auric Field, or The Energetic Body. Those hunches you're getting are direct results from your Energetic Body checking in with the other energies around you.

When you think of charismatic speakers who can project a field that others entrain to, they can captivate a room and bring everyone to hold the same vibration because all the energetic fields are synching up. On a bigger level, people who can manage their field really well with a dominant centering, these include our charismatic speakers, popular politicians and cult or terrorist leaders. They can project a field that others will entrain to.

For me, I use Vibes Up products to support my energy field. My field is particularly sensitive to Wi-Fi, and the Vibes Up bracelets and shoe inserts help insulate me from the effects of Wi-Fi. I have several vibes Up Pyramids, too. I never travel without them, and I keep them around all the electronics in my home. Interestingly, one application of Vibes Up never occurred to me—while I was out of town, my son had to take care of a friend who got ridiculously drunk. And then, the next morning, my son had to take care of a friend who was ridiculously hungover. In that hangover state, the friend asked my son for the "pyramid thing" to make him feel better.

Hoarders surround themselves with static energy that will eventually overwhelm them by simply creating stagnation as a dominant field. Your environment affects your energetic field in this way. If there's no space for more blessings, the universe can't send you more of what you want. We live on a plane about vibration. It's common that a lot of empaths feel drained, simply from lack of information on how to manage their sensitivities safely and comfortably. Today I generally keep my vibration high (through thought, emotion, intention and vibes up) so that I don't entrain down around others. You, too, can keep a high vibration by using principle-based thinking, which includes learning how to manage your energy to have the best experience of you.

If you have a healthy liver, it vibrates higher than an unhealthy one. If you're happy you feel bubbly and light; in grief, you feel like an elephant is sitting on you. We do know that there are higher frequencies of health. Live food like salads and fresh juices are a higher vibration than cooked or highly processed foods. Yet, both can be beneficial to your bodies. I've realized that a healer doesn't heal a person—they hold such a cohesive state of higher vibration that others can entrain to it and feel better. When you're vibrationally cohesive, other bodies can reorganize at that higher frequency, heal, and be healthier, without your resonance lowering.

The idea here is to hold your own frequency high and avoid entraining down. Think about a day when you feel wonderful. You feel good for no particular reason. You get a call from a friend who feels very low and down, and she really needs to talk to you. At the beginning of the conversation, your vibration is high while theirs is low. Although, by the end of the conversation, your vibration has sunk while theirs has risen. They thank you for making them feel much better, and yet you're feeling so drained that you need either Starbucks or a nap. What happened? You entrained to each other.

Ideally, you want to be able to hold your frequency such that you can help others come up to your high vibration without entraining down. As mentioned earlier in the book, Cesar Milan is an excellent example to illustrate this point as the Dog Whisperer. He holds a high vibration and trains the dogs he works with to entrain up instead of being stuck in fear, and aggression. Bring consciousness to your vibrations in order to raise them. Where do you feel good? Do you notice how you feel, not only with how you eat, but also with what you think, feel, and what you're around? In what environments do you feel better or worse? How can you support that body? Stand outdoors and in nature or wear vibrational technology.

Spiritual Body

This body is your connection to something bigger than you. If you don't believe in something bigger than you, or that you're a complex being with separate energies, you can have trouble healing, especially if you have a lot of health issues. While the 7 bodies are all interwoven, your Spiritual Body connects to everything at all levels of being, to your soul self, ancestors, other dimensions and realities, and the one Divine Intelligence that is the Creator. The Spiritual Body is my connection to everything, and I am limited in human consciousness for how much I can perceive of everything that is in existence.

For some students, this is the most difficult body to understand, yet it's the simplest to describe. If you've ever wondered what New Age philosophy means when they say they're connected to everything, they are referring to their Spiritual Body.

Karmic Body

Your Karmic Body is the inherited or past life patterns that were passed down to you. This is how musical ability or artistic ability runs in a family in the same way that limiting beliefs can do so. We can participate in family patterns that repeat, often without realizing it's happening. In simple terms, this can be things you probably want less of like: hereditary diseases, addiction, violence, or financial scarcity, and then you want to look at finding and changing what's not working for you.

One major determiner of your Karmic Body is your parents, and I mean this in terms of nature and nurture, or both DNA and parenting or how they set the example. Some metaphysical leaders say we pick our parents, although I didn't exist as I am now before I came in. I didn't attract my parents either, which is something else you might have heard. The person I am now didn't choose this life for me, good or bad. No one would choose addiction or chronic pain, so choosing your path is more complex than that. This is your epigenetic or karmic energy that's from your ancestors in your DNA or from previous soul experience. Like, did you come in with a fear about money or not?

Your Karmic Body is the aspect of you (the soul self) that wanted to explore different experiences on Earth. What spiritual leaders mean by "you picked your parents" is that the aspect of you that is closer to God, in a different dimension, wished for different experiences to explore on Earth.

When you're trying to address a painful past, it can feel like victim blaming to hear that you chose your experiences, including being a victim of a crime or abuse. To come out of victim consciousness, it's more helpful to consider how there's something bigger than you going on and, in a different reality, this bad thing that you experienced was a good choice for your karmic self. My Karmic Body was created from a divine plan that gave me the female gender, made me straight instead of gay, gave me this personality, and set me into my particular family dynamic. It's more generalized and less personal.

Be loving and kind to evolve your Karmic Body without judgment and resistance to what is. Whatever genetic coding and personality type you have, don't get stuck there. Use every challenge to evolve into a strength. In a football game, a player has to run across the field with a ball, and the other players want to stop them, there are penalties. If all you had to do was run across the field with no obstacles, no one would want to play. It's the game of trying to run with the ball despite the obstacles that makes the point significant. Even with pain or limited abilities, you get to use what you have and play the game of life anyway.

And, remember that humans rarely feel fulfilled unless they've had a challenge. We admire those who persevere in spite of overwhelming obstacles, and your Karmic Body is often choosing those struggles that allow you to shine as your best self in the face of difficulty.

Egoic Body

The Egoic Body is the aspect of humans that allows us to feel separate and individualized. Its job is to weigh, measure and compare. Today for the first time we can literally evolve the ego to serve our spirituality. Weighing, measuring and comparing our choices and growth for positive outcomes instead of the old way of ego criticizing and painfully judging. When setting a goal, it's the ego that is utilized to keep schedules and assessment of what is working or isn't. Often in spiritual growth clients forget to use the ego for logical support in changing a pattern they desire to evolve into something else.

Putting It Together—*Cindy*

I had the most trouble figuring out my Auric from my Emotional and Karmic bodies. This caused me to look at some of the times in my life when I had blamed my emotions, but maybe there was something more going on energetically or epigenetically.

My previous boyfriends were truly decent gentlemen who meant me well, although they were also deeply wounded. I think that's what had attracted me to them, and I had wanted to fix them. It was a curse of the "all I need is a good woman" theme from literature and even soap operas. I wanted to save them and make them into who they wanted to be. At 27, I took a serious look at my life and decided to make the change not to date another boy seriously unless he was already in a good place. I also played the TLC song, "No Scrubs," a lot.

At that time, in 2007, I only knew what I learned from Rhonda Burns on *Oprah* about energy, and nothing about genetics outside Punnett's Squares. With my new insight into the bodies now, I looked at my transformation to understand it better.

I had been right to shift my emotional and mental bodies from expecting someone broken to expecting someone whole. And, I had decided that I was worthy of the love and attention from such a man. Something else happened too, though. When I would tell friends and family how I went from dating losers to dating a successful engineer and marrying him, it always felt like something else was missing. I wasn't explaining the other changes I had made, which I didn't even understand.

A lot of women I know have married their dads, and a lot of them aren't happy about it. I don't want to call my father a loser, although I will say he was not ambitious in life the way I would have hoped. In many ways, his refusal to accept leadership positions in the church and community and his contentedness to never pursue a promotion in more than 20 years impacted my ideas for my own success and that of my future partner.

Looking back, I saw that I had transformed the energy around success that had held me back from even flirting with established, powerful men before. In doing so, I must have changed the energetic legacy of my family line somehow, altering my Karmic Body. I wondered if I might have even affected my father, who had already passed away two years before, yet whom I always felt was right with me, and still do to this day.

There was a lot more to understand, and I couldn't wait to have Helen help me put it all together.

Post Notes—*Helen*

I suggest that you start thinking about all 7 Bodies by doing a check-in the next time an uncomfortable feeling or thought pops into your head. What body do you think it's coming from? Notice what happens when you address that body. It's tough to interrupt a pattern that's not serving you when you don't know where it's coming from, and it might feel natural or inevitable, although you get to decide how you feel and what you do about it. Try it out. Look for the LLOA Spiritual Planner on my website to give you more information on using your bodies proactively for conscious co-creation.

CHAPTER 16

TOOLBOX

Wrapping Up—Helen

In this final chapter, I leave you with a few tools that can help you trouble-shoot your process when you feel stuck. I know that in the beginning of the book I talked about how tapping, on its own, wasn't giving me or my students everything we needed to get clear and stay clear, although that doesn't mean it can't be a great tool to use alongside your energy work and principle-based thinking.

On the way to developing LLOA, I've had success with a lot of different energy clearing modalities, even though I understand the process now to be energy transformation. I want to share a little bit about them with you. I refer to them in this book in passing because they are already great books and resources you can seek out if you're interested to practice them.

Tapping and EFT

According to its founder, Gary Craig, tapping clears energy glitches. Craig teaches you to tap on endpoints of meridians in the body while you focus on a negative belief, thought, relationship or circumstance, thereby releasing the congested energy that is causing a glitch in your system.[16] You might benefit from a tapping session if you feel like you

---

[16] You can find out more at Craig's website www.emofree.com.

should feel better than you actually do. Tapping may also be helpful when you aren't making as much progress as you want.[17]

When I'm in the "shoulds," I use EFT because I'm in a painful emotional loop. Tapping while I focus on my judgments clears enough space for me to be in choice.

Students of LOA are sometimes hesitant to try EFT because it requires them to call up negative thoughts and emotions. I believe that when you're engaging the negativity through validation, instead of resistance or suppression, you soften and sometimes completely transform them. Energy is transformed when you're in the old energy and show up differently. Plus, the added benefit of tapping is that it makes you be present.

However, tapping will only take you so far. While it can help you focus on and clear the energy glitches that are stalling your progress, tapping can't give you the new information you need to have different results. The underlying issue(s) that caused the glitches are energetic patterns, which can reappear until you recognize, address and transform them. The transformation is done by using principle-based thinking to show up in the old energy pattern and do things differently.

Access Consciousness

Another tool for clearing energy is Access Consciousness. This system is based on the energetic bars in your head that correspond to different life experiences. Practitioners strategically stimulate those areas to release limiting beliefs and negative energy, and you say clearing statements to clear illusions and lower frequency thoughts.

---

[17] I also encourage you to check out the over 2,000 categorized taps in my EFT Audio Library at www.helenracz.com.

It amazes me that even today after all my tapping, I still find limiting thought-patterns to clear with Access.

This method was the first energy clearing modality I found in 2003, and as a young mother, I practiced Access on my kid's heads a lot. Other mothers noticed that my sons had drama-free lives, and when they asked me what I did, I suspected that it was Access (in addition to raising them with principle-based thought consistently). This is a great tool when you're trying to clear blocks from your mental, karmic, and emotional bodies.

Journaling

I began gratitude journaling after reading Rhonda Byrne's *The Magic* and continue daily because of the huge payoff I've seen in my life. I also wrote endless forgiveness statements, and it made a big difference in clearing the energy around some of my old wounds. As a bonus, like tapping, journaling forces you to be present because when you're writing, you can't multitask or check out.

Forgiveness

A lack of forgiveness can block your progress, expansion or growth. If you're in gratitude—generally choosing love over fear, taking right action, finding information, and having support systems in place—and you're still stuck, then you may need to ask whether you're withholding forgiveness. You will know you need forgiveness work if you have memories that trouble you. If other modalities don't work, look to work with forgiveness.

Forgiveness is an energy of coming out of victim-consciousness and suffering. It isn't yet well-anchored on Earth. It's about separating yourself from the energy connection to persons or events that you believe make (or made) you feel bad. I've done Radical Forgiveness worksheets and really benefited from reading them aloud, which is part of the process. This helps you be free of lower vibrations and attachments to people and past experiences.[18]

Apply What, Why, How, and How You'll Know When You're Successful

Applying the "what," "why," "how," and "how you'll know you're successful" questions allows you to utilize your mind as a tool with imagination, visualization, and clear intention for alignment to who you'll be once you complete all necessary action steps. "What" asks for the specific issue you want to address—your end in mind. "Why" asks for your internal motivation at the deepest level to bless you, others, and the planet. "How" asks for the practical steps you're going to take to create consistent action that changes the old pattern to a new one. "How you'll know when you're successful" asks for benchmarks you can use to compare your results to your original end in mind.[19]

There is one more level of alignment in mind, heart, and action. Consciously focusing on imagining the future version of you is very powerful. Athletes do it! There is science on using the mind to create health, fame, and skill. People envision future businesses, buildings, weddings, restaurants, and movies, all before they take shape. It helps them stay on course and engage others into supporting the creation. Use the gift of your imagination and seriously get a feel of yourself in the future, when what you now desire is simply the norm.[20] What's different? What's the same?

---

[18] For more information, you might check out *Radical Forgiveness* by Colin Tipping, as well as my *Forgiveness Tapping Workbook* available at www.helenracz.com.

[19] Check out my book, *Tell Me Where You're Stuck*, for a deeper dive into this toolset, along with helpful guiding examples.

[20] I created the *Joyous Intention Setting PDF* for you at www.helenracz.com to help you think through this alignment.

When you practice consistently, and often enough that you feel a strong emotional connection with your target, you successfully align and evolve yourself into the energy of positive expectation (faith). It's very nice when you find yourself in full belief without the pressure of worrying about the timing. That is successful alignment.

Here's an example I created to show you how you might work on integrity. I include this because I am surprised at how little this in included in LOA teachings. Without integrity you seriously limit your ability to have the results you desire:

- **The What**: Improving integrity. It means alignment with truth as you know it. Speaking your truth when appropriate and taking action to follow through consistently means you are integrous in word and action.
- **The Why**: Integrity is about order and the energy of clarity in thought and action. It's also about consistency, which is a big factor here on Earth for creating anything, positive or negative. (Think of brushing your teeth or eating fast food; both must happen regularly to affect results.) It's all about the compound effect. Lack of integrity in any area is often about unfinished business—promises made and not kept, debts left unpaid, commitments unfulfilled, betrayals and secrets that are never made known and resolved through apology and right action. Incompletion can be a pattern that limits the conscious creation of a desire.
- **The How**: Keep your word consistently and always. Go back and finish anything left incomplete. If you speak it, then follow through with it or literally make your change known. Show up on time and fulfill your commitments and intentions. Know your ethical code, your defined honesty, and live it fully.
- **How You'll Know You're Successful**: Your actions will match your thoughts and words. You'll have less chaos in

relationships and schedules because you'll be dependable and trustworthy. You'll get more done with less effort.

Are you getting the idea? Let's try another one for Forgiveness:

- **The What**: All negative emotions lead back to fear, and forgiveness brings freedom from fear of the past repeating. Fear separates us from good. Love connects us to good. Forgiveness is an energy that frees us from negative emotional patterns, inner pain and often physical pain! Forgiveness is still a new and unusual energy here on Earth, yet it is becoming more a part of humanity and will create peace within and around you. Forgiveness is never something that is simply done and over; it is a choice that we may keep making for freedom from victim consciousness and limitation.
- **The Why**: The refusal to forgive limits your capacity for good. It is about negative judgment, which separates and isolates from expanding good. Forgiveness is the exact opposite. It liberates you from victim consciousness and empowers you to choose and connect with more good!
- **The How**: There are different ways to access the energy of forgiveness and anchor it in your life and consciousness. Many times, it takes an expanded paradigm spiritually to stay the course. What story or teaching do you believe about life and the pain and suffering you experience here? Energetically there are tools like Ho'oponopono and Radical Forgiveness (you can find information online) that transform situations and relationships through the use of forgiveness energy. Writing out forgiveness statements 70x7 times can expand your ability to let go of energetic ties to old pain of the past.
- **How You'll Know You're Successful**: You will feel good more often than not! Painful memories will no longer be controlling your thought patterns or actions. Your stamina for happiness will expand, and you will know it. Being present will be more the norm and easier.

You can follow that same simple outline and design your own pathway for whatever you want most. For success in any endeavor, all old beliefs that don't fit what you want to experience must come to surface to be evolved. Follow the same rule for everything you want to change: Show up in the old energy and think, act, and speak differently. Stretch your skill in faith (positive expectation). Evolve disappointment into positive expectation. Fear into love. Doubt into self-confidence. Anger into clarity. Evolve resentment and blame (lack of forgiveness) into freedom. Sadness into closure and new possibilities. Failure into new solutions. Worry into gratitude. Everything changes in a positive way after the challenge of choosing your thoughts, feelings, and actions with principle-based thinking.

Achieve Harmony

The evolutionary state we can reach for today is to know and experience ourselves in love; a challenging endeavor because fear has kept us (humans) alive when we existed in survival mode and fear contributes to our exploration as individualized beings. Now those of us reading a book like this have the opportunity (in one short lifetime) to evolve rapidly in our consciousness—aligning to love at levels that were not possible before.

Expanding the energy of love would create harmony with mind and heart, and with spirit and form, as it is the consciousness of Heaven on Earth. On the way to learning about love and how we can choose to experience ourselves, we face many complex levels of our beings. In this process, tapping is a good tool, as is hypnosis, meditation, Vibes Up, medicine, nutrition, surgery, energy work, vibrational therapy, and more—although, none of these tools give you the full package of true harmony through love. This journey isn't about an end game of perfection, ease and grace; this is about the process of living and exploring and developing the skill of choice. Could you consider learning to love the ability, and challenges, of developing skill in choice of thought, word and action? Skill that gives you the means to evolve love into your natural way of experiencing yourself and life here on Earth, even in the most painful of times?

You don't create your whole reality. You don't control disease or the economy or any of the other challenges you face in life. The one thing you control is your experience of you. As I mentioned when we talked about the Karmic Body, I disagree when people say you create your own reality. If that was true, there are enough of us that we would have healed the planet of all its ills by now. No, you can't create your entire reality because you can't one-up God, and you're on a planet with billions of other people who are also busy creating. We are part of the whole.

However, we can choose our perception of reality and how we respond to it.

The most powerful vibration for positive change is love. When you get to know more about the complexity and levels and layers in yourself and in life, you can begin to expand your consciousness to see the love in the organization of the Divine Plan. It's a choice to believe in a loving Creator. A choice to become the loving personal creator of the inner peace and happiness you desire. Learn how to engage with yourself to create a powerful self-love. Your level of self-love is in exact proportion to how much love you can give the world and receive from life and others. Know it's a continuous journey of choosing —there is never an endgame while here in this dimension. Can you imagine falling in love with the endless opportunities to transform fear into love? Can you imagine falling in love with your humanness because it is the catalyst of evolution and expansion?

Understanding how the Law of Attraction is Logical helps you to see and evolve any pattern that has painfully prompted you to pay attention to it. We are so much more complex than we know, and learning all you can helps you continue evolving. Want to be good at math? Start with the basics and keep adding to your knowledge base. It's the same with understanding how to perceive your reality and to align yourself with what you wish to be and receive. Choose to love yourself enough to work with the Logical Law of Attraction, by knowing how to think so you consistently have the best experience of you. Choose to do so, because you can.

> *We begin exploring self-growth and metaphysical teachings to get the things, circumstances, and relationships we believe will give us happiness. That beginning is putting the cart in front of the horse.... once we focus our minds on feeling love, success and gratitude Right Where We Are, consistently, we eventually live the reality of those feelings in our 3D world, like a book becoming a movie. Lyrics becoming a song that moves thousands of fans. Like a story that elevates generation after generation. Like a seed that grows into a tree. It truly is as within, so without.*

APPENDIX A

A LITTLE ABOUT HELEN

My family came from England to America when I was four. We became US citizens when I was seven. I was exposed to the drug culture early on. Without any core self-esteem, I had many difficult and dysfunctional relationships, even marrying at 19 and divorcing at 21. I had no sense of who or what I wanted to be or what to aim for.

Then, in 1987, the Universe literally rear-ended me into a new chapter through three pivotal events: chronic pain from whiplash in a car accident, reading Melody Beattie's *Codependent No More*, and meeting Greg. The car accident happened when I had no insurance, so my new norm was financial stress on top of needing medical guidance to heal my body. I was introduced to biofeedback and self-hypnosis at a chronic pain center in Houston in 1987. After the accident I ended a relationship and was living on my own, working retail for a very low salary. In an attempt to better my life, I began working a second job and started at the Art Institute of Houston. Then, due to my hands going numb, I dropped out of the Art Institute after one semester.

Beattie's book had opened my eyes; I realized I was a stereotype (so embarrassing!), and I could learn from books to transform my life in a positive way. I've never stopped seeking and reading. The part-time job allowed me to meet Greg. We've been married since 1989 and I think of my life story in terms of "before Greg" and "with Greg," with the latter being my journey into health and joy. The chronic pain led me into entrepreneurship for income, and meditation for relief.

Both our sons are fertility babies, meaning it was a long arduous project getting pregnant, and there were also a few early miscarriages. My tailbone broke in the first delivery; more pain and challenge for my body.

I always give credit to Sean, my second child, for propelling me on this journey of spirituality. He was born so incredibly angry. It was astounding the intensity of his emotions. I believed that level of anger could make his life incredibly challenging in many ways- ours too! I was determined to find answers to help my son. I did find answers: teachers, energy workers, and protocols that led me into EFT, teaching, coaching and even channeling. There are stories within stories in my life of how I evolved myself, yet those are another book in itself. Or, catch me sharing stories in interviews on YouTube by searching for Helen Racz interviews. I have a playlist on my channel.

The point is, I came from a place of years and years of fear and mental stress, emotional pain, physical trauma and underlying anger and sadness that I felt was my norm. Thus, I was motivated by pain to find answers and direction. I broke the cycles of anger, violence, addiction and low self-esteem in my family line through my commitment to positive change. Today, I am all about learning how to evolve into a thriving consciousness through joy and love, which is very different than pain motivation! I know who I am, what I am, and how I serve. And, with Cindy, we choose to be of service through the sharing of the Logic of Vibrational Law so that you can use it to your benefit.

APPENDIX B

CINDY A YEAR LATER

"I asked my boss to find more work for me to do locally so I don't have to travel so much," Jack told our friends. I almost fell out of my seat.

We were having dinner at Maggiano's in Houston's Uptown area with Heather and John, a couple we've known since we lived overseas.

"I thought you traveled a lot," Heather said.

"I used to. Now I mostly consult on international projects."

Wow. I had noticed that my husband had traveled less over the past few months, but he didn't tell me that was his choice. This year, my husband is spending Christmas at home, but he'll probably be offshore in the Gulf of Mexico for New Year's. At least I get him for one holiday.

When I wrote the Foreword about doing the holidays alone, I couldn't predict the long-term effect I was having on my husband. I couldn't "make" him change his job, and what I could do was be supportive and kind so that I was a vibrational match for him to want to be around me more and care not to leave me alone.

I've also completely changed my business—including charging higher rates, not working on the weekends or into the evening to spend more time with my husband, and taking time to write my book, articles, newsletters, presentations, workshops, and a mini-course. All of which, I couldn't be doing so well if I was still all worked up about not already being "successful."

And the last time a friend brought up that other person who had been a literal "pain in my neck," I was able to listen and be supportive, without reacting with my own emotions. They didn't come up at all because I was able to keep my bodies aligned with my intention to keep a high vibration, regardless of what's going on with her and the other people who choose to still associate with her.

I can't change her, but I can change how I react to her, and that makes me happier and less distracted by drama so I can focus on the relationships and goals I care about.

With the ability to shift my energy around writing and not being so attached to the when and how, I'm able to be consistent in the 7 habits and trust that I'm creating my best experience of myself, as Helen would say.

APPENDIX C

GLOSSARY

These are definitions for terms as they are presented or used in this book.

- **7 Habits**: Steven Covey coined the term "Habits" for the principles he uncovered while studying success of individuals, groups, and businesses throughout history. The 7 Habits in Stephen Covey's book *The 7 Habits of Highly Effective People* are: (1) Be Proactive; (2) Begin with the End in Mind; (3) Put First Things First; (4) Think Win-Win; (5) Seek First to Understand, Then to Be Understood; (6) Synergize; (7) Sharpen the Saw.
- **Altered State**: An altered state of consciousness or mind is significantly different from a normal waking state and can be measured as types of brain wave patterns through technology as Beta, Alpha and Theta. It describes induced changes in one's mental state, almost always temporary.
- **Energetic Body/Auric Field**: See *Body, Energetic/Auric Field*.
- **Belief Systems**: A belief system is an ideology or set of principles that helps us to interpret our everyday reality. This could be in the form of religion, political affiliation, philosophy, or spirituality, among many other things. These beliefs are shaped and influenced by a number of different factors.
- **Body, Egoic**: The ego gives us the experience of being separate. Its job is to weigh, measure and compare. Some earlier spiritual or psychological teachings suggest the ego

must be eliminated. Today, I believe we can evolve the ego to serve our heart and soul.

- **Body, Energetic/Auric Field**: The sixth sense feelings you get about other people or spaces come from your Auric Field, or The Energetic Body.
- **Body, Emotional**: Your Emotional Body is invisible, though you have a range of emotions that you feel in your Physical Body. Everyone does. Human beings have the self-awareness to feel your emotion and then align it to an action that is chosen versus instinctual reaction.
- **Body, Karmic**: Whatever it is that makes you different and unique from other people—from small things like wearing glasses or having a special way with animals to big things like traumatic experiences, being paralyzed, your personality, repeating patterns in relationships with self, health, money, others, career, etc. These are what you have come to explore.
- **Body, Mental**: In popular psychology, the mind or Mental Body is often broken into the conscious, unconscious, and subconscious. All three of these consciousnesses comprise your Mental Body, which, if developed properly, can become an invaluable tool for your progress.
- **Body, Physical**: Your Physical Body is the physical manifestation of your dominant vibration. This includes your karmic energy, genetics, dominant emotional patterns, and thought patterns because the Physical Body holds all this information. It also expresses your emotions physically.
- **Body, Spiritual:** The Spiritual Body, in contrast to the natural body, is the immortal body and spiritual element of conscious understanding of being connected to all that is. This body is your connection to something bigger than you. While the 7 bodies are all interwoven, your Spiritual Body connects to everything at all levels of being—to your soul self, ancestors, other dimensions and realities, and the one divine intelligence that is the Creator.

- **Channeling**: Channeling is a means of communication through a specific frequency for which humans choosing to channel become a conduit.
- **Circle of Influence:** Circle of Influence is a term Covey used to describe concerns that we can actually do something about.
- **Clarity**: The quality of being intelligent and coherent in our thoughts and actions. Clarity is about awakening yourself to being present and to being someone who co-creates purposefully.
- **Conscious Creation**: Conscious creation is when you choose to work with the universe on multiple levels to co-create your reality on purpose with purpose.
- **Conscious Mind**: See *Mind, Conscious.*
- **Dominant Resonance**: The most consistent pattern of all the frequencies from your past, genetics, outside influence, thought patterns, emotional patterns, environment, and beliefs either inherited or co-created. Your dominant resonance is your natural unconscious default mode.
- **Drama Trauma**: When you are in reaction mode, dealing with drama that adds more trauma through your thoughts and actions.
- **E's:** Helen's affectionate term (nickname) for the Emissarians.
- **EFT (Emotional Freedom Technique(s))**: See *Emotional Freedom Technique(s) (EFT).*
- **Emissarians (E's)**: The Emissarians are a stream of consciousness, and also an aspect of consciousness reached through channeling.
- **Emotional Body**: See *Body, Emotional.*
- **Emotional Freedom Technique(s) (EFT)**: Emotional freedom technique (EFT) is an alternative treatment for physical pain and emotional distress. It's also referred to as tapping or psychological acupressure. Created in 1990 by Gary Craig.

- **End in Mind**: Have a high level of clarity for what you are intending to accomplish for all your individual goals and your overall life's work.
- **Energetic Legacy**: We all come in with this energy from our ancestors, like a genetic legacy for skin and hair color. The phrase, "the sins of the father," does apply, and then children are all different, so everyone in the family doesn't have exactly equal parts of each bit of inheritance. And we create, pay forward, our energetic legacy for the next generations through our thoughts and actions.
- **Entrain**: This is the mechanism by which you either increase or decrease your vibration to be a match with something else.
- **Epigenetics**: A means in which trapped emotions can be passed on from one generation to the next and how the predisposition to a specific mental or emotional imbalance does have epigenetic origins.
- **Four Questions (Four-Part Formula)**: The four questions of conscious creation: The What, The Why, The How, and How You'll Know You're Successful.
- **Frequency**: The rate at which vibration occurs i.e. a "high vibration" vibrates at a high frequency, and a "low vibration" vibrates at a lower frequency. You might think about a radio frequency to envision how vibrational frequencies operate, showing up through receivers that extract the information.
- **Genetics**: The genetic properties or features of an organism, characteristic, etc. that are handed down to offspring.
- **Karmic Body**: See *Body, Karmic*.
- **Law of Attraction (LOA)**: The law of attraction is the attractive, magnetic power of the Universe that draws similar energies together. It manifests through the power of creation, everywhere and in many ways. Even the law of gravity is part of the law of attraction. This law attracts thoughts, ideas, people, situations and circumstances.
- **Logical Law of Attraction (LLOA)**: Applying principle-based thought to the Law of Attraction (LOA).

- **Mass Consciousness**: The big soup of everyone's thoughts and emotions, in which the most dominant thoughts are those with the strongest patterns.
- **Mental Body**: See *Body, Mental*.
- **Mind, Conscious**: The conscious mind directs your focus, distinguishes between real and imagined thoughts and stores short term memories.
- **Mind, Subconscious**: The subconscious stores short and long-term memories for recall and influences actions and feelings.
- **Mind, Unconscious**: The **unconscious** mind stores repressed and automatic memories, and although these memories can be accessed with effort, they usually run in the background undetected.
- **Mission Statement**: A formal summary of the aims and values of a company, organization, or individual.
- **Physical Body**: See *Body, Physical*.
- **Principles**: The principles that operate in physical expression are called natural laws. Principles are fundamental truths and also referred to as spiritual laws that work across all time, cultures and generations.
- **Resonance**: Two vibrations at the same frequency will "resonate" or harmonize together, and this is how it's said that "like attracts like."
- **7 Bodies**: Also see: *Body, Energetic/Auric Field*; *Body, Emotional*; *Body, Karmic*; *Body, Mental*; *Body, Physical*; *Body, Egoic* and *Body, Spiritual*.
- **Spiritual Body**: See *Body, Spiritual*.
- **Spiritual Laws**: Spiritual laws are constant, unchanging and essential for creating balance and harmony.
- **Subconscious Mind**: See *Mind, Subconscious*.
- **Tapping**: A nickname for EFT. Tapping is a combination of Ancient Chinese Acupressure and Modern Psychology that works to physically alter your brain, energy system and body all at once. The practice consists of tapping with your

fingertips on specific meridian points while talking through traumatic memories and a wide range of emotions.

- **Unconscious Mind**: See *Mind, Unconscious.*
- **Vibration**: Science tells us nothing is solid, there are always atoms moving and there is more space than matter. Everything is energy, seen and unseen, and in its most basic form energy is a vibratory pattern. The nature of the pattern determines the frequency.
- **Vibrational Law**: Everything vibrates, both physical and metaphysical; this includes emotions and ideas, as well as objects, and they all vibrate at different frequencies.
- **Victim Consciousness**: Victim consciousness is a stage of consciousness in which people deny personal responsibility for the things that happen in their lives. People in victim consciousness believe that the world is acting upon or against them, and they are the innocent targets of other people's action or behavior.
- **Vision Board**: A vision board is a tool used to help clarify, concentrate and maintain focus on a specific life goal. A vision board is any sort of board on which you display images that represent whatever you want to be, do or have in your life.

APPENDIX D

FURTHER READING

I suggest some of these books and websites within the chapters and included other resources that have helped on my journey so you can quickly find good information:

Recommended Books

- *The 7 Habits of Highly Effective People* by Stephen R. Covey
- *The 7 Habits of Highly Effective Teens* by Sean Covey
- *Conversations with God* by Neale Donald Walsh
- *The Magic* by Rhonda Byrne
- *Power of Now* by Eckhart Tolle
- *Power vs. Force* by David R. Hawkins, M.D.
- *I Am Word: A Guide to the Consciousness of Man's Self in a Transitioning Time* by Peter Selig
- *Your Soul's Gift: The Healing Power of the Life You Planned Before You Were Born* by Robert Schwartz
- *Language of Emotions: What Your Feelings Are Trying to Tell You* by Karla McLaren
- *It Didn't Start with You: How Inherited Family Trauma Shapes Who We Are and How to End the Cycle* by Mark Wolynn
- *Bridging Science and Spirit; Common Elements in David Bohm's Physics, The Perennial Philosophy and Seth* by Norman Friedman

Digital Resources

- Helen Racz: www.HelenRacz.com
- Emissarians: www.emissarians.com
- Cindy Childress: www.ChildressCommunication.com
- Gary Craig: www.EmoFree.com
- Gregg Braden: www.GreggBraden.com
- Jarrah Hewitt: https://jarradhewett.com
- Joe Dispenza: www.DrJoeDispenza.com
- Julie Parker: www.YourInnerBlueprint.com
- Karla McLaren: www.KarlaMcLaren.com
- Meaning to Pause: www.MeaningToPause.com
- Passive Brain Fitness®: www.PassiveBrainFitness.com
- Radical Forgiveness: www.RadicalForgiveness.com
- Vibes Up: www.VibesUp.com
- Spectrum Center: https://spectrumcenter-houston.com

Printed in the United States
By Bookmasters